AF661356

# ROLE CONFLICT AMONG WOMEN TEACHERS

# ROLE CONFLICT AMONG WOMEN TEACHERS

Shakuntla Devi

Commonwealth

**Role Conflict Among Women Teachers**

© Shakuntla Devi

Edition **2022**

ISBN 81-7169-918-9

*Published by* :
**COMMONWEALTH PUBLISHERS (P) LTD.**
4831/24, Govind Lane,
Ansari Road, Darya Ganj,
New Delhi - 110002
Ph. : 23272541, 23242541
e-mail : commonwealthpublishers2016@gmail.com

*Distributed by* :
**ARJUN PUBLISHING HOUSE**
4831/24, Govind Lane,
Ansari Road, Darya Ganj,
New Delhi - 110002
Ph. : 23272541, 23242541
e-mail : arjunbooks2001@gmail.com

*Laser Typesetting by* :
**Dimple Computers**
Delhi

*Printed at* :
**Milan Enterprises**
Delhi

# Preface

The well-known French Utopian Socialist Charles Fourier, who developed a system of ethical socialism once said, "One can judge the degree of civilization of a nation by the social and political position of its women". The status of women in a society is the true index of its cultural, social, religious and spiritual levels. The status of women varies greatly from state to state and even between various communities in a particular state. For instance in Kerala and in Meghalaya the society is matriarchal whereas in the rest of India society is partriarchal, Hence women in Kerala and Meghalaya have much greater rights, are free, enjoy more privileges and respect than women in other parts of India. It presents a shocking paradox. Though praised sky high theoretically, they are worst hit practically. A number of social and religious customs taboos, inhibitions, rituals etc., prevail in Indian society which come in the way of women's freedom, education, work participation and also other spheres of life.

Besides this, women especially in rural areas perform multiple duties by combining all types of household chares including child-care with such jobs as farming, animal husbandry, word in household industry etc.

The position of women in Haryana is no better than their counterparts in the rest of the parts of the country. No doubt within a short span of its existence Haryana has assumed an important place in the economic attainments of the country. But it is rather unfortunate that this material prosperity could not go along with its moral commitment to enhance the status of its women. Change of attitudes is really slow and is markedly reflected in the low sex-ratio, literacy, education, participation in employment and training and high mortality rate for females, growing demand for dowry and highest rate of suicide by women due to dowry disputes, tension and depression, conflicting situations arising outside and inside of their physical and mental set-up etc.

In order to remove the hovering discouraging environment and apathetic feeling of men towards women and to create a sense of security and equality among women, the Indian Government tried to gear up and activate official machinery. Consequently several research bodies at the level of University and similar organizations have been created to examine intricacies, problems and other social facts which preclude the behavioural implementation of social economic and legal equality of women.

Above all, discrimination against boys and girls must die at the earliest, Both boys and girls have to be brought up in a genderless milieu so that their impressionable minds are kept chaste and uncontaiminated by the pollution of sexism. This would involve not only discarding of sexist undertones and overtones from the ideologies, mythologies, text books etc., but also a process of self appraisal and analysis on the part of parents, teachers and administrators etc. Once this has been done, this process would lead to role amelioration. When roles would no more be rigidly defined in terms of musculiarity and feminity the very roots of sexism would be chopped and hence would result in the estremination of the oppression of women. The birth of the daughter would no longer sink the hearts of the parents and dampen the spirite of the near and dear once. In this regard my worthy teacher Dr. Neshla says : *"Hardly matters; if it happens to be a daughter or a son, Both provide to the life its meaning, its beauty and fun. Look : Daughter embodies glory, grateness and grandeur. Be proud of her, why deprive thyself of that loving splendour?"*

The famous English Play Wright William Shakespeare has said, "Frailty the name is woman". Jai Shankar Prashad, a well-known Hindi Poet called her "Abla" Tulsidas has regarded "Women inferior to man". At the same time realizing the potentialities of women She is called 'Shakti', 'Durga', 'Goddesss' and 'Lakshami'. Constitutionally, she is equal to man but in practice she is denied all rights. This paradox compelled me to think about the factors which are responsible for this worse situation of women.

For instance, UGC has set up special cells for women in a number of Universities and also directed for the same in colleges by the State. It is obligatory on their part to take up some research and developmental programmes for women. It will be better if these women cells run in the rural areas also. It is the fact, problem of this sort is more aggravate at grass-root level. Hence, development ptogrammes taken up in general at National, State and District level will be treated as merely throwing arrows in the darkness. Therefore, an idea of shaking the conscience of the society and to sensitise its slumbering souls that there is a need of deeper probing into the problem of incompatibility of roles faced by women teachers working in urban as well as rural areas of Haryana State.

I hope social scientists, researchers and other academics in the concerned discipline, this work will be of utmost use.

Words fail me to express my deep sense of gratitude to Professor C.L. Kundu, Ex-Dean Faculty of Education, Professor Y.P. Aggarwal, Ex-Chairperson, Department of Education, Professor S.M. Gupta, Chairman, Department of Education, Kurukshetra University, Kurukshetra, for their valueable suggestions, co-operation and assistance in the present work.

I also feel indebted to Professor S.P. Malhotra and Professor N.S. Mavi (both Ex-Chairpersons), Department of Education, KUK who inspired me to write and get publish your work during their expert-talks at C.R. College of Education, Hisar. Their valueable guidance kept me on the writing track.

My Heartfelt thanks are to Professor Neshla, Department of Education K.U.K. and also to Mr. T.C. Saini Ex-Principal DIET Mattersham (Hisar). Who provided me their constant encouragement and valueable suggestions. My sincere thanks are to Sh. R.P. Dagav, Librarian, C.R. College of Education,

Hisar who inspite his duty schedule was good enough to provide Library help from time to time. My grateful thanks are due to the library staff of H.A.U. Hisar, NCERT, NIEPA Delhi, Harya Secretariat, Chandigarh and Kurukshetra University, Kurukshetra for their kind help.

I am greatly inspired by Dr. R.S. Dalal, Chairperson, Department of Education, CDLU, Sirsa who suggested me for the publication of independent work. I am indebted to Dr. (Mrs.) R. Sood Reader, Department of Education, KUK for her sympathetic, painstaking and timely guidance at every step of investigation and report writing, without which this work would not have been possible for me to accomplish and disseminate well to all.

I am thankful to my colleagues and friends who appreciated my work and encouraged me to do move from time to time.

Last but not the least my thanks are to Sh. K.C. Sharma and publisher M/s. Commonwealth Publisher, who helped in its wider dissemination through this novel series at present.

**Shakuntla Devi**

# Contents

# List of Tables

# List of Figures

# 1 Introduction

## 1.1 WOMEN IN VARIOUS PERSPECTIVES

From Ahilya onwards to the present times, the historical epochs have witnessed immense rise and fall in the conditions of women. May it be home or office, factory or farm, sowing field or scavenger site-her role has always been prominent especially from the work point of view in almost all the times.

Dating back to vedic age, a woman enjoyed equal rights of living with her male counterpart. However, she had to pass through deteriorated conditions by becoming dependent on her father, brother and husband and son in her life span during different other periods. This deplorable conditions of woman remained unchanged throughout the Hindu period. The Muslims too looked down upon woman as inferior to man folk. Her declined status was reflected in the customs regarding marriage, religion, property, widowhood, dowry, role in the family alongwith other basic attitudes with respect to the social image. This position was prevalent in the early years of the British Period. But after sometimes, the spread of English education and intermingling of western and Eastern cultures enabled the Indian woman to realize and regain her legitimate status.

In the wake of time, educated women came forward demanding equal rights with men. They also raised their voice for enhancing the status of women during that period. As a consequence of their struggle, an awareness was created in the society and a tangible reformatory suggestion was in the form of involving woman in some economic activity.

The advent of the second world war resulted into some

important changes in socio-economic status and social relationships. The United Nations Organisations reaffirmed faith in the fundamental human rights, in the dignity and worth of the human beings and also in the equal rights of men and women.

The Indian Reforms Act of 1921 included women as a part of it. After the first World War, Mahatama Gandhi set the pace for the progress of Indian women in all spheres of life. He also advised them to emancipate themselves from drudgery of the kitchen.

Post independence period brought much success to women who till now were striving hard to get their due. Many drastic changes in women's work and family roles brought about tangible implications for employment and family policy. The trend of women working outside their home started with these important events :

*(i)* The freedom movement which brought the women out in struggle for material liberation leading to independence and the Constitution which guaranteed equal rights to all citizens including women.

*(ii)* The report of the committee on the status of women in India (SWI 1974) which made the first assessment of women and focussed on her as 'individual' with rights of her own.

*(iii)* The UN Women's Decade which influenced women's thinking all over the world and forced governments to shift the emphasis of womens' programmes from welfare to development.

Both in cities and villages, women are taking more and more jobs by breaking the social-psychological barriers. They are doing so not only for the sake of improving the standard of their families but also because of hard economic necessity (Myrdal, 1956). They are employed as teachers, doctors, lawyers, nurses, engineers, journalists, officers in the government departments as well as in non-government sectors. Her entry into forces and para military departments has opened novel vistas of her changed roles. A cursory look on the data depicting women in the world of work will be interesting as well informative.

## 1.2 TREND OF FEMALE WORK PARTICIPATION

Indian women whether urban or rural make substantial contribution to national economy. Ironically in Indian society the work undertaken by the women is not considered in economic terms by the family as she is not recognised as economically productive. Her image of a householder included the work of housewife alongwith the provider of food and comfort to the family.

Eighty per cent women of the third world are the providers of essentials like food, fodder, water etc. (Verma, 1992). The two lakh villages of Indian would have remained waterless, if onus of fetching water had been left to men. The valuable services rendered by women to keep the house-fires burning have so far gone uncomputed. An average woman of the third world works for 18 hours a day. However, they are recipient of less food, health care, education and productive assets.

Traditionally, Indian women have assisted their better-half in rural areas in sowing, harvesting, tilling etc. In fact, in agricultural contribution of woman is about seventy five per cent.

In 1988 National Commission on self-employed women reported by Sharam Shakti pointed out that 87 per cent of our women work in unorganised sector, whereas in the organised sector, women constitute only 13.3. per cent of all the employees. In the public sector they account for 11 per cent of the total employment and in the private sector for 17.8 per cent.

It is estimated that 75 per cent of women in the organized sector (9.9 per cent) continue to work as unskilled, low status, low prestige, dead end jobs, such as mid-wives, clerks, teachers, nurses, at meagre pay.

The work participation rate in the country excluding Jammu & Kashmir, indicated that more than a third of our population is working. Among males, more than half are workers while among females only one in four to five is engaged in some kind of work.

**Table 1.1. Total workers in India, 1991**

| *Popualtion/Workers* | *Persons* | *Males* | *Females* |
|---|---|---|---|
| | **Total** | | |
| Popualtion | 836,605,522 | 433,791,705 | 402,813,817 |
| Workers | 314,903,642 | 223,506,153 | 91,397,489 |
| Percentage of workers | 37.64 | 51.52 | 22.69 |
| | **Rural** | | |
| Population | 621,267,297 | 320,062,940 | 301,204,357 |
| Workers | 249,330,072 | 167,822,985 | 81,507,087 |
| Percentage of workers | 40.13 | 52.43 | 27.06 |
| | **Urban** | | |
| Population | 215,338,225 | 113,728, 765 | 101,609,460 |
| Workers | 65,573,570 | 55, 683,168 | 9,890,402 |
| Percentage of workers | 30.45 | 48.96 | 9.73 |

The work participation rate is higher in the rural than in the urban areas. The percentage of total workers in the rural areas among the total workers in the country is 79.18 while the percentage of the population living in rural areas is 74.26. Sex-wise 75.09 per cent of the male workers and 89.18 per cent of the female workers in the country have been enumerated in the rural areas. Whereas 73.78 per cent of the male population and 74.78 per cent of the female popualtion in the country have been counted in these areas.

There has been a considerable increase in female work participation rate during all these years. Participation of women in various types of work has direct bearing of their level of education. Both education and employment are inseparable.

**Table 1.2. Work Participation Rate in India, 1971-1991**

| *Year* | *Total/Rural/Urban* | *Males* | *Females* |
|---|---|---|---|
| 1971 | Total | 52.75 | 14.22 |
| | Rural | 53.78 | 15.92 |
| | Urban | 48.88 | 7.18 |
| 1981 | Total | 52.62 | 19.67 |
| | Rural | 53.77 | 23.06 |
| | Urban | 49.06 | 8.31 |
| 1991 | Total | 51.56 | 22.73 |
| | Rural | 52.50 | 27.20 |
| | Urban | 48.95 | 9.74 |

**No. of Literates 1991 (Haryana)**

| *Rural* | | | *Urban* | | |
|---|---|---|---|---|---|
| *Persons* | *Males* | *Females* | *Persons* | *Males* | *Females* |
| 4,939,138 | 3,386,087 | 1,553,051 | 2,492,570 | 1,486,670 | 1,005,900 |

It can be worked out that the percentage of literates in rural and urban areas is 66.46 per cent and 33.54 per cent respectively. Further, amongst the literates in rural areas 68.56 per cent constitute males and 31.44 per cent females. On the other hand urban literates consist of 59.64 per cent males and 40.36 per cent females. The male literacy rate is relatively high (67.85%) in the state as compared to female literacy rate (40.94%) which was also true for the country as a whole.

The role of woman as a school teacher is important as she makes noteworthy contribution in the holy task of building the future of India.

The number of primary schools is 537,000; middle schools 1,37,000 and secondary schools 69,000 in India (Report of Ministry of Human Resource Development 1988-89).

**Table 1.3. Number of Teachers (Annual Report 1988-89)**

| *Sr.No. Category* | *1950-51* | *1986-87* |
|---|---|---|
| 1. Primary schools | 5,35,000 | 15,22,000 |
| 2. Secondary schools | 85,000 | 9,79,000 |
| 3. Secondary/Highers Secondary schools | 1,27,000 | 11,99,000 |
| Total | 7,47,000 | 37,00,000 |
| **Percentage of Female Teachers** | (%) | (%) |
| Primary schools | 15.3 | 30.56 |
| Upper Primary schools | 15.2 | 32.18 |
| Secondary schools } | 15.7 | 28.12 |
| Hr. Sec. Schools } | | 29.33 |
| **Percentage of Trained Teachers** | | |
| Primary schools | 58.2 | 86.66 |
| Upper Primary Schools | 53.3 | 87.33 |
| Secondary Schools } | 55.5 | 90.23 |
| Higher Sec. Schools } | | 88.55 |

These figures serve as an eye opener as her number in various places of work are increasing day by day. She is considered as potential contributor towards the national economy.

## 1.3 WOMEN AND HER MULTIPLE ROLES

The job role of a woman also coincides with her family role. And in between these two roles she obliges social patterns set by the society. If one carries out single handed all the duties of home and job, one experiences stresses and strains. If on the other hand, one does not carry out efficiently one's dual role, one feels accused of being inefficient and vain, and suffers from guilty conscience and finds herself torn between home and work. If this situation is left uncontrolled and undirected, it may lead to disorganisation of family and society of which women form an integral part.

Multiplicity of roles is inevitable among women teachers

which creates confusion regarding the performance of roles. This cycle of role conflict goes on between expectations of others and expectations by oneself. Sometimes there is a problem between two roles which happen simultaneously and for other times there is conflict due to the expectations attached to a single role. One thing should be considered that expectations always vary from person to person and also from time to time.

## 1.4 CONCEPT OF ROLE CONFLICT

Role can be described in many ways depending upon the situation in which it is to be performed.

Jones and Gerad (1967) take role as a "behaviour that is characteristic and expected of a person who occupies a position in the group".

Role may be said to be a "pattern sequence of learned actions or deeds performed by a person in an interaction situation" (Sarbin, 1954). The concept of role conflict is the outcome of those situations when conflicting situations due to dual or more roles occur.

Role conflict occurs in certain situations *i.e.* the actor or role player is required to fill simultaneously two or more roles that present contradictory expectations. And it is impossible for an actor to conform to those conflicting expectations. That is what usually happens when a woman has to perform simultaneously roles of a housewife and a teacher. In this context, Linton (1945) and Goffman (1961) state that because of different personality characteristics and dispositions, the role conflict may became noticeable in women.

Role conflict is the term which has generally been used by sociologists and social-psychologists to refer the problem situations which arise due to simultaneous roles. The degree of conflict depends upon the nature of circumstances. Goode (1960) denoted the role conflict by role strain or role stress.

Thus, role conflict, role strain, role stress all are concerned with the same sense-due to which problems arise for the individual as a result of role incompatibilities or two or more simultaneous roles. (Sinha 1988) (Goode 1960) (Kahn 1964). Role conflict may be categorised in the following way :

*(a) **Inter Role Conflict :*** It occurs when a person occupies two positions simultaneously (Sarbin 1954).

*(b) **Intra Role Conflict :*** It occurs from a number of sources within a specific role (Nye, 1980).

Both inter role conflict and intra role conflict have pivotal place in every day schedule of working women as these lead to conflicting situations causing them enough harassment.

## 1.5 ROLE CONFLICT IN WOMEN TEACHERS

A woman teacher, besides occupying the positions of a housewife and mother, also holds the position of an employee. Therefore, as compared to non-working housewives, a woman teacher has to perform a number of roles *i.e.* the role of a mother, a wife, a daughter-in-law and a social person fulfilling her obligations towards the society. And on the other hand, she also acts as a teacher at her work place *i.e.* school. She has to perform more than one role simultaneously for instance, besides her duties as a teacher she has to act as a subordinate, a colleague, a head of the institution and so on.

In addition to her usual jobs, a woman teacher being a working wife has to discharge a number of duties and responsibilities related to her specific roles. Sometimes, these duties and responsibilities might be antagonistic and incompatible in nature. The performance of these responsibilities and roles give rise to role conflict. The conflict experienced by professional woman having a family, stems not simply from participation in two different activity systems whose claims on time allocations are incompatible. The conflict derives from the fact that the values underlying these demands are contradictory in nature. A professional woman is expected to be committed to her work "just like men" at the same time as she is normatively required to give priority to her family (Coser, Rose, L., 1961). After all, men are fully engaged in their professions and occupations without fearing and without being told that they are not committed to their families. It can be precisely said that this commitment on the part of men, is main driving force for their hard work. Hence, one does not think of working men as having a conflict between their family and occupational obligations. The conflict may arise due to normative and conflicting expectations. The action may be incompatible physically, socially or psychologically as with rise in status, the number and diversity of obligations as well as the number of role-partners tend to increase, and this goes to multiply the number of expectations. Therefore, a married teacher is compared with a non-working housewife on conflicting role expectations, it may be considered that a woman teacher has to tackle with more conflicting role expectations. So, it is felt that a woman teacher experiences greater conflict between her family roles and job roles because of the antagonistic and incompatible nature of the roles.

## 1.6 JUSTIFICATION OF THE STUDY

It has become an uphill task for working women in all fields in general and for women teachers in specific to cope with the changing societal demands in reference to their multifaceted roles made upon them. Interestingly, they are involving in discharging more than a singular role in their day-to-day schedule and as such it becomes arduous for them to decide as to how much time is to be devoted towards which role.

For instance a women teacher working in a school has to comply with her family obligations which are obviously more than that of her male counterparts.

Role conflict can also be explained in terms of the condition of body and mind forcing tensions, stress and frustration. This arises in women teachers because of profuse societal expectations and their inability to take proper decision in those complex circumstances. One of the most dangerous trends among working women including school teachers is that they are on the way to stop the right of claiming custodianship of their children alognwith other family members. It is thus obvious that her motherhood is being deteriorated by receiving challenges from her "busy woman".

Another problem of working woman is her exploitation by the head of the institution and other male colleagues. At times, she is harassed for petty gains over minor matters. Most of these women do not get enough physical and emotional supports from their respective husbands and in-laws and that is why their woes have become incessant.

On one hand she serves in the school environs whereas on the other she also acts as mother, wife, sister, daughter etc. in her family. The problems of working women further aggravate as they have to work in the environs which are totally different from those of their own home. Distant places of work also cause considerable inconvenience to working women. This verifies sources of such problems which worsen woman's status due to low salaries, lesser chances to promotion.

Further, there are a number of problems arising due to compatible and multiple obligations which a woman teacher has to fulfil alongwith other demands of the society. Sometimes she considers her home role as prime one whereas other times this becomes secondary.

It has been rightly pointed out that women are often their own enemies. Mother-in-laws and sister-in-laws often try to poison the man's ears. This type of difficulty is also faced by our women teachers in their family life which creates obstacles in their way.

Ahmad (1979) reported that attitudes of husbands, wives and parents are marked by ambivalence. Working women find it difficult to combine the dual roles of a housewife and mother on one hand and that of a working women on the other. Role conflict occurs due to conflicting expectations of others. Further it was observed that women obstruct the path of women more than men.

The message is also left to convey that nobody has tried to motivate our women teachers to strike out all the meaningless customs and traditions.

Being a teacher, woman cannot farry out efficiently each

of her roles as a wife, mother, teacher, housewife and social being. Many times, she suffers from guilty conscience and finds herself torn between home, school and society. For instance, when her husband and other family members do not cooperate and change their attitudes and behaviour, she becomes more tense. Her family and social life suffers in marital disharmony and marital frictions. This condition creates social and psychological problems. Meanwhile she faces inter and intra personal problems thrice that is at home, school and society also. Some problems related to her job take place such as while working with men she considers herself isolated if she is of a reserved nature. But on the other hand, people take her flirt, if she is of friendly nature. Sometimes, she comes under the suspicious and annoying attitude of her husband being working with her male colleagues.

A teacher can teach well if she is happy and satisfied. Teacher is the key figure in the life of nation. She should be of cooperative nature and possess a sound personality. But due to stress and strain in one's roles, it is difficulty to perform one's role efficiently in any sphere of life. The members of no other profession are so intimately involved in the task of improving the nation as the teacher is. Hence, the adjustment or maladjustment of a teacher significantly affects her home roles, job role and social role. All this lays an indelible impact on the nation in general and society in particular to which she belongs. Due to the burden of various roles on the mind of the woman, she faces enormous problems discussed above at length.

This study was a deliberate attempt to study the nature and extent of conflicting situations due to their changing role of working women teachers in their family, job, society etc. It will also investigate the relationship of some variables like level of education, location, management of school, type of school, teaching experience, marital status, socio-economic background and type of family. Besides this, this work will also investigate the relationship of role conflict with various personality factors. For the sake of studying role conflict among working women teachers a role conflict scale will be constructed and standardized. Overall, this study will revolve round the following questions :

Which of the personality factors contribute to Role Conflict among working women teachers? Whether educational qualification of a teacher lays some impact upon the role conflict in working women teachers? Whether married working women experience more role conflict as compared to their unmarried counterparts? Whether women teachers working in rural areas face more role conflict than their colleagues working in urban areas? Whether women teachers working in co-educational schools experience more conflict as compared to women teachers working in girls and boys schools? Is there any impact of type of family on role conflict? Whether women teachers serving in government schools face more role conflict as compared to their counterparts serving in private schools and aided schools? Whether working women teachers having more than five years of teaching experience prone to more role conflict than their counterparts having less than five years of teaching experience? and whether socio-economic background of women teachers has an influence on role conflict they experience?

Thus, the title of the thesis can be described as :

## 1.7 TITLE OF THE THESIS

"A study of socio-psychological correlates of conflict between family role and job role among women teachers".

## 1.8 OPERATIONAL DEFINITIONS OF THE TERMS USED CONFLICT

Glueck states that "Conflict is said to exist between two or more individuals or work groups when they disagree and clash over a significant issue, or a number of issues".

The following two categories of role conflict are considered in the present study :

*(a)* ***Inter Role Conflict :*** It occurs when a person occupies two positions simultaneously; and

*(b) Intra Role Conflict* : It occurs from a number of sources within a specific role.

**Role**

It is a pattern of feelings, beliefs, attitudes, values and behaviour that a person in a particular social status is expected to exhibit.

Sarbin (1971) defines role as a "patterned sequence of learned actions or deeds performed by a person in an interaction situation".

Ogburn (1979) defined that "a role is a set of socially expected and approved behaviour patterns consisting of both duties and privileges, associated with a particular position in a group".

**Rolc Conflict**

It is the situation in which an individual is expected to play two or more different roles that involve responses that are competing or antagonistic, and thus cause role conflict.

In the present study, role conflict of women teachers of Haryana will be studied regarding various, roles performed by them namely family role, job role, social role, dual role etc.

**Family Role**

The obligations of a woman rendered towards her family constitute her family role.

**Social Role**

The group activities and casual interaction of individuals in their respective society outside their homes.

**Working Mothers**

A mother of minor-age children who is employed outside the home in either part-time or full time work.

**Woman Teacher**

A woman teacher engaged by an educational institution to instruct (Hawes and Hawes, 1982). Both J.B.T. and B.Ed. women teachers were included in the perview of this study.

## 1.9 OBJECTIVES OF THE STUDY

1. To construct and standardize a Role Conflict Scale (RCS) for women teachers.
2. To study the nature and incidence of Role Conflict among women teachers.
3. To study the socio-psychological correlates of role conflict among women teachers with respect to personality factors, socio-econonmic-status, educational level, matrial status, type of the school, location of the school, management of the school, type of family and teaching experience.
4. To find out the differences of Role Conflict experienced by women teachers with respect to their educational level, marital status, type of school, location of the school, management of the school, type of family and teaching experience.

## 1.10 HYPOTHESES

The following null hypotheses were framed to realise the aforesaid objectives of the study.

1. The role conflict among women teachers is not normally distributed.
2. There do not exist significant relationship between role conflict and various socio-psychological correlates such as personality factors and socio-economic status with respect to educational level, marital status, location of school, type of family, teaching experience, financing and management of school and type of school.
3. There do not exist significant differences in the mean scores of role conflict experienced by women teachers with respect to their educational level, marital status, location of the school, type of family teaching experience, financing and management of school and type of school.

## 1.11 DELIMITATIONS OF THE STUDY

1. The study is delimited to 360 women teachers randomly drawn out from the State of Haryana.
2. The study is delimited to study the role conflict experienced by women teachers included in the present work.
3. The study is confined to two socio-psychological correlates *i.e.* personality factors and socio-economic status.
4. The study is conducted under the light of following variables *i.e.* educational level, marital status, location of the school, type of family, teaching experience, financing and management of school and type of school.
5. Only inter-role, intra rolc, family rolc job role, social role and dual role conflict were included under the perview of this study.

# 2 Review of Related Literature

Survey of related literature is the foundation stone of research. Hence, it is advantageous to survey the work which has already been done in a particular field. It also furnishes the investigator with a necessary sequence of knowledge in the concerned field. It also helps the investigator to have a clear comprehension of the research studies already conducted to have an idea of the subject of the study in all aspects and implications. Avoiding the work of duplication, it reveals the facts, which had remained untouched, unexpected and unexplored in the previous researches.

The study of related literature acts as a guide post, not only in regard to the quantity of work done in the field but also enables the investigator to perceive the gaps and lacunas in the concerned field of research.

Before finalizing a research proposal, may be in any field, it is the survey of related literature which proves of paramount assistance in the entire gamut of methodological steps.

The exercise of reviewing studies provides essential information on the related work already available in that field while avoiding unnecessary duplication. It also helps revealing the facts and figures which has earlier remained untouched, unexpected and unexplored in the previous research studies.

The study of related literature is important as it acts as a lighthouse not only with regard to extent of work done but it also enables investigator to perceive the gaps and lacunas in the concerned field of research. In simple terms, survey of related literature means to locate, to read and to evaluate the past as well as the current literature of research concerned with the project undertaken.

Therefore, the study of related literature can never be ignored in any type of research. To quote C.V. Good, "Without a critical study of the related literature the investigator will be groping in the dark and perhaps uselessly repeat work already done". So to save one's human and non-human resources, one should undertake a detailed and penetrating study of all the literature available.

The main purpose of survey of related literature is not merely compilation but an analytical review of the various study sources. The related studies stimulate and encourage the investigator to go deep into the intricacies of the problems and also enables to derive respective conclusions.

In the light of the significance of the related literature, it was indispensable for the investigator to conduct a survey of the related literature.

For convenience, two below given broader classifications of related studies were made :

## 2.1 STUDIES CONDUCTED ABROAD

*(a)* Studies related to role conflict.

*(b)* Studies related to the working conditions of professional women including teachers, and

*(c)* Studies related to personality and allied attributes of professional women including teachers.

## 2.2 STUDIES CONDUCTED IN INDIA

*(a)* Studies related to role conflict,

*(b)* Studies related to the working conditions of professional women including teachers, and

*(c)* Studies related to personality and allied attributes of professional women including teachers.

## 2.1 STUDIES CONDUCTED ABROAD

### *(a)* Studies Related to Role Conflict

Grace (1974) carried out a study to analyse the assumptions made by Wilson on the teachers' role. The major objectives of the study were that which groups or categories of teachers have significantly higher perception of conflict in the teaching situation and which groups have significantly higher personal experience of them. A sample of 150 secondary school teaches was taken in a Midland town and his investigation focussed attention on intra role conflicts.

The findings of this study were mainly that role diffuseness was not a major source of role conflict. Teachers with more than 10 years of teaching experience perceived significantly more conflict than less experienced teachers.

Organ and Greene (1974) studied role ambiguity, locus of control and work satisfaction among scientists and engineers employed in an electronics firm. Data were collected through questionnaires such as Rotter's Internal-External Control Scale, a measure of role ambiguity and job satisfaction measures. The study concluded that locus of control was related to both role ambiguity and satisfaction.

Nevil and Demico (1975) and Johnson and Johnson (1976) focussed their studies on Role Conflict in women as a function of marital status. It was taken with regard to family size and other aspects of role conflict, that is human relations. Data were collected from the women and mothers of the state through role conflict questionnaires. An analysis of the data found that a woman felt stress when she became mother and stress goes on increasing when she had a large number of children. It was also supported that motherhood is overloaded with stress (Shaw and Costanzo 1970).

Miles (1977) examined role set configuration as a predictor of organizational role stress experienced by 202 research and development professionals representing 5 organizational roles. Organizational distance and relative authority of role senders were taken as the dimensions of role-set. Results of the study revealed that the organizational distance and relative authority of role senders were found to be important predictors of specific types of role conflict and ambiguity.

Abdel-Halim (1978) carried out a study on employee effective responses to organization stress among managerial personnel of a company in the mid west. The relative importance of role conflict, role ambiguity and role overload as sources of stress and dissatisfaction among managerial staff was taken as the objective of the study. The study revealed that the role ambiguity had the strongest relationships with role responses in the predicted directions. Significant interactions were obtained between levels of role ambiguity and role overload, but not between the levels of role conflict and job characteristics.

Halehan and Gilbert (1979) carried out a study on inter-role conflict experienced by career and non-career oriented working women. The purpose of the study was to find out the correlates of role conflict and contribute stress among working women with children. Data were collected through role conflict questionnaires from married and working women. The results found that variations in spouse support, work commitment and the nature of job situations contributed to the extent to which married working women with children experience role conflict. The job group reported much less satisfaction from their work roles from their family roles.

Abraham (1986), Savery (1986), Burke and Greenglass (1987), Michaels; Day and Jocachimsthaler (1987) conducted their respective studies to examine perceived excessive stress among employees. Some of them concentrated their studies on the interface between the work and family life. One fourth of the sample reported that they often experienced stress. Role ambiguity and role conflict were noted as major stressors. It was also concluded that job interference mediated the effect of time demands on satisfaction, organisational commitment and psychological strain. Role overload was also perceived as a major stressor for some respondents in the sample. Role conflict was found to be associated with lower work satisfaction.

It can be concluded that role conflict and role ambiguity are caused by the role overload and multiple roles. Role ambiguity is associated with lower work satisfaction.

Robinson and Skarie (1986) and Newton and Keenan (1987)

carried out their studies on professional women and role stress predictors respectively. Inter-relationship among the internal variables of locus of control (LOC), fear of success (FOS) and sex-role traditionality and their relationship to women's external job role stresses were examined. Findings of the study suggested that greater the respondent's internal LOC, the less her perception of role overload, role ambiguity and non-participation in work situation was. Results supported the relevance of personal, interpersonal and organisational predictors to role stress. It was also suggested that role stress research differentiated between varying forms of role stress that is role conflict, role ambiguity, quantitative overload and quantitative underload.

Mckenry *et. al.* (1987) surveyed 150 rural employed mothers to determine family and job predictor of satisfaction with the dual work role. Data were collected in respect of expectation of working, education, support for working from significant others, job satisfaction, reasons for working, autonomy and sex role modernity. The findings of the study suggested that saliency of job satisfaction variables in determining role satisfaction among this group as opposed to hypothesised group. The results were discussed in relation to the importance of employment outside the home to life satisfaction, particularly for mothers of older children. It was also found that a women experienced problems in dual role since household responsibilities and child care had greatly diminished during that time.

Tremaglio (1987) conducted a study to investigate the relationships among principles and perceptions of their role conflict and ambiguity and the perceptions of their teachers regarding principal effectiveness and teacher morale. The sample constituted principals and teachers of schools. Data were collected through questionnaires. Pearson product moment correlation indicated to significant relationship between principal role conflict and any aspect of principal effectiveness. Teachers' perceptions of principal effectiveness were related to most aspects of teacher morale that is rapport with principal, other teachers, teacher work load, teacher status satisfaction with facilities, and community pressures.

Koberg and Chusmir (1991) worked on sex-role conflict in sex-a-typical jobs. The study was aimed to know female-male differences on Sex Role Conflict Scale. The sample constituted 80 females and 86 males. The findings supported that placement in a job dominated by the opposite sex did not have a significant relationship to the level of sex role conflict. It was concluded that subjects may experience reduced conflict between the self-perception of their role and the roles expected of them in their role and the roles expected of them in their professional lives.

Tipping and Farmer (1991) conducted a study campaign career counselling implications. It was aimed to assess women's conflicts resulting from home and career values as incompatible. The sample was constituted of 97 single college women enrolled in a large mid-western University. The subjects were completed both the Home-Career Conflict Measure (HCCM) and the Attitudes towards Sex Roles scale (ASR). The results and supported that HCCM scores were significantly related to the traditional sex role attitudes measured by ASR (Attitudes towards Sex Roles scale).

Barnett and Marshall (1992), Goldberg, Greenberger, Hamill and O' Neil (1992) carried out their studies on employed mother and mother roles. The major objectives of the studies were to examine the relationship between the occupancy and quality of multiple roles and psychological distress. The results revealed that variables reflecting the interface between work and family roles were important for both women's well being and perceptions of children's behaviour. It was also found that depression appeared to be more closely related with the stability and resources in single mothers' lives. Role strain was also affected with the time, energy demands of the work and level of the support available to the subject.

Borg and Riding (1993) carried out a study to investigate the relationship between the teacher's cognitive style and occupational stress in State Secondary Schools in the Maltese

Islands. The data were collected through self-administered questionnaire. Teacher's age, teaching post, school selectivity, single sex school and curriculum subjects taught were organised in one's respective manner. The results of the study were reported that the overall level of self-reported teacher stress was evenly distributed in the cognitive style groups.

The studies have shown that an employed mother, employed woman teacher experienced role strain, role conflict which was affected by time, energy, demands of the work and support. It was also concluded that teacher stress was evenly distributed in the cognitive style groups. Dual role conflict was significantly related to traditional sex roles attitudes, time factor and motherhood.

### *(b)* Studies Related to Working Conditions of Professional Women Including Teachers

Vogev and Brett (1985) and Barnett and Baruch (1985) conducted their studies related to interest in the work—non work interplay. The considerable attention was paid and focussed on conflict between work roles and other roles. Familial roles were taken in particular. The study revealed that conflict between job and off job roles may produce strain, dissatisfaction with the job. It was also concluded that conflict between work and non work activities may result to reduction in organizational commitment.

Greenhaus and Parasuraman (1986) examined the intersection of work and non work roles as related to stress and its consequences. The theory proposed an integrative framework for understanding the relationships among stressors, stress and strains in the work and non work domains. The sources and consequences of work—non work stress were reviewed. Personal and social influences on work—non work stress were identified. Individual and organizational strategies for effective management of work—non work stress were described. Butler, Sandra and Wintram (1991), Covin Teresa and Brush (1991).

Moradi (1987), Phelps (1987), Nhundu (1987) carried out their respective researches on work place conditions, background variables, role ambiguity and their impact on job satisfaction among school teachers. Data were collected through questionnaires and interview methods. Specific conditions identified as student motivation, behaviour expectation, salary, emergency home leave, major medical insurance child care, multilingual instruction. The study revealed that there was no statistically significant difference in job satisfaction attributable to school size and level, and gender of respondents. The work related problems of English teachers were not limited to the classroom level and most frustratively perceived problems occurred on the school and community levels.

Seidman (1989), Carpenter (1989) conducted their respective studies to examine the responses of dual career couples about employment and career situation of women. The data were collected regarding to attitudes of spouses relevant to their family and career roles. The model couple in the study was married 6 years, upper middle class with fewer than two children and working more than 40 hours per week. The findings of the study recorded that wives scored higher than husbands on family role behaviour. Husbands and wives scored similarly on inter role conflict, marital adjustment and number of hours worked per week. It was supported that age, location and health care were found to be critical barriers to their personal and professional development.

Ganser (1989) conducted a field based study on high school teachers of academic subjects teaching in a large urban school system during the year 1987-1988. Data were collected through interviews in a variety of situations. The ideas of each subject about good teaching and the work of good teachers were noted. An analysis of data showed that students provided greatest influences on the subject's ideas about good teaching in relation to their staff and their working conditions. Overall, the subjects' beliefs about good teaching remained intact after their first year of teaching experience.

Barcinas (1989) conducted a study to compare the attributes of rural and urban secondary schools and twelfth-grade students in Ohio. The main purpose of the study was to examine the differences between rural and urban schools. This correlational study consisted of rural schools and urban secondary schools. The results indicated that relationship between educational and occupational aspirations and the characteristics of rural and urban schools were not significant.

Webster (1991), Scott (1990), Abdulmatlul (1991) carried out their respective studies regarding demographic variables and socio-demographic variables such as marital status, age, number of children, levels of education, income, and experience among women in the labour force. The main purpose of the study was to investigate patterns and trends of female employment and the structure of the labour force in relation to occupational differentiation on the basis of sex. Hence, data were collected from female workers. The findings of the study showed respondents' education and age were the most important variables that determined her occupational status. The study also concluded that wives did significantly more than husbands in the areas of household tasks and child care. It was also supported that couples' sex role identity scores were significantly different, they had no significant effect on the wife's career commitment. Women's wages were found to have a significant positive effect on marital quality.

Hamilton (1990) conducted research to identify combinations of variables that most affect well being among employed women. Data were collected from a national sample of married employed women representing dual employed families. A hypothesized model of stress, and copying process examined the influence of situational demands on mediators and mediators on well being. Job and family strain as well as coping strategies and coping resources were proposed to mediate between situational demands. Results of the study suggested that both role strain and coping resources mediated the stresser effects of situational demands on well being.

Rice (1990) conducted a study to examine the transition of new comer teachers from Pacific Rim countries. The sample of the study constituted teachers having teaching experience in elementary or college level educational institutions in their native countries. Data were analysed using a critical hermeneutics framework and the work of Haus-Georg Gadamer and Paul Ricacur. The newcomer teachers reported experiences pertaining liminality, communities, and fusions of horizons in three general domains, that is the culture, new school environment, and within their classroom.

Steffens (1990) constituted a case study design to examine the perceptions of the National State Teacher of the Year in relation to specific conditions and characteristics of effective teaching and learning. The study examined the characteristics of teacher effectiveness, classroom methodologies and demographic information. The findings of the study indicated that most important characteristics necessary to the effective are knowledge of subject matter, a caring and compassionate personality, enthusiasm, organization, a sense of humour and a love of children.

Eichinger, Heifetz and Ingraham (1991) carried out a study on women teachers in special education to find out correlates of work satisfaction and learn out stress among women teachers. Social role orientation was measured by Bem Sex Role Inventory for each subject. An analysis of data showed that a balanced social role orientation on the job was associated with higher levels of job satisfaction and lower levels of job stress.

Hatta and Nishiide (1991) conducted a study on Japanese primary teachers' stress. The purpose of the study was to compare the levels and characteristics of several facets of stress in primary school teachers with those of white collar workers in private companies. The study revealed significant interactions between several groups and stress factors. Primary school teachers (PSTs) experienced greater subjective stress mood than white collar workers (MCWs). It was also found that white collar workers experienced greater stress regarding their future prospects than primary school teachers (PST's).

McCormick, John and Robert (1992) carried out their project on teachers' attributions of responsibility for occupational stress and satisfaction. The data were collected from 387 teachers in terms of occupational stress and occupation. The results of the study showed an association of occupational stress with job satisfaction. It was also found that there exists significant differences for biographical variables such as sex, type of school and location of school (Seidman and Zager 1991).

Glass and Camarigg (1992) explored a study regarding gender, parenthood and job-family compatibility among employed women. Data from male and female subjects were collected. It was found that gender segregation appeared to worsen females' working conditions rather than making mothers' lives easier.

Strickland (1992) worked on institutional norms and role satisfaction among employed wives. The objective of the study was to compare the Assemblies of God Missionary Wives (MWs) with other types of career wives. Data were collected through participant observation, interviewing, analysis of documents and questionnaire research on 200 Missionary Wives (MWs). The findings suggested that Missionary wives often evoked satisfaction in response to institutional emotion norms. It was also found that unlike other types of career wives, Assemblies of God Missionary Wives (MWs) reported very high role satisfaction and low depressive symptomology.

Chilman (1993) published an article which summarised related research regarding the impact of Parental Employment and child care trends. There was emphasis on recent developments regarding federal legislation that is Family Support Act 1988. It looked at the pros and cons of parental full-time employment versus—part-time-stay-at-home parenting. Finally, some suggestions were outlined for charges in current norms and values, as well as in public and private policies. Issues for poor people were emphasized. It was also suggested that child-care problems might be lessen by employee assistance programmes and by family sensitive employer policies. President Clinton signed the act into law in February 1993.

The studies support that knowledge of subject matter, love to teaching compassionate personality, income and working environment contribute to effective teaching. The school and community problems contribute to frustrations on the part of teachers. These also follow that biographical and demographical factors bear significant relationship on the level of job stress.

### (c) Studies Related to Personality and Allied Attributes of Professional Women Including Teachers

Frommer (1986) carried out a study on Australian government employees to work out systolic blood pressure (SBP) in relation to occupation and perceived work stress. Data were collected through a questionnaire. The study revealed that there was an association between systolic blood pressure and occupation. It was also found that age, occupation, body was index and level of perceived stress arising from financial problems were significantly related with systolic blood pressure.

Coleman (1987) conducted a study to investigate the relationships between personality traits and job satisfaction among music teachers. The major objective was to measure the patterns of personality traits that were common among music teachers. The sample constituted 107 experienced music teachers. California Psychological Inventory (CPI) was used to investigate the personality traits. Correlation coefficient was used to determine the relationship between job satisfaction and personality traits. The study supported that there was no significant relationship between personality traits and job satisfaction.

McClain (1987) designed a study to investigate the relationship between personality characteristics and teaching effectiveness of secondary vocational agriculture teachers. The objective of the study was to examine the relationship between the personality type characteristics and teaching effectiveness of teachers. The Data were collected on a stratified random sample of 193 secondary vocational agriculture teachers. To examine the relationship between personality type characteristics and teaching effectiveness, an analysis of variance was conducted. Significant differences were found to exist on personality indicates when compared with the teaching effectiveness.

Guyton (1987) carried out a comparative study of the personality traits of secondary science teachers in mississippi public schools. The purpose of the study was to identify the personality differences between outstanding science teachers, regular certified science teachers and provisional certified teachers of science. The hypotheses included that there was no significant difference existed in the personality traits of the three groups of science teachers. The data were collected through Cattell's 16 Personality Factor Questionnaire. The results of the study supported that the outstanding teachers group was more abstract thinking, self reliant, realistic and independent. They were also more resourceful, preserving, proper, moralistic, rule bound, aggressive and preferred hard working people in witty companions.

Quinn (1987) conducted a study on cognitive style, personality and classroom management of special education teachers in non-public schools. The study was designed to investigate the cognitive and personality styles and good classroom management of 40 special education teachers. Myers-Briggs Type Indicator was used to measure personality characteristics. The subjects of the study were divided into categories of field independence and field dependence. The study unexpectedly found a strong relationship between introversion and good class room management especially for men. It had also shown that special education teachers alongwith elementary teacher are generally extroverted.

Green (1987) designed a study to determine whether spousal age difference affects the status of American women, relative to their husbands and to each other. The respective objectives were made in respect of age differences, race, socio-economic background, educational attainment at marriage, age at marriage and number of children. The analysis was based on data from National survey of family growth and American women aged 15-44 were selected. The study found that women older than their husbands were more likely to be better educated and to have nigher likely to be better educated and to have higher status occupations and higher incomes, compared with other women.

The studies quoted personality traits, cognitive style and socio-economic status of teachers and working women. The studies supported that outstanding teachers are resourceful and hard working. The special education teachers and elementary school teachers are generally extroverted.

Morris (1989) carried out a research on women's well being. The sample contained all mothers aged 40-49. Half of the women were married and half were divorced. Quantitative and qualitative data were collected through questionnaires and interviews. Mastery and pleasure, two well being factors were identified. Mastery consisted of measures of higher self esteem, locus of control, self role quality balance score and lower depression. Pleasure consisted of measures of life satisfaction, happiness and optimism the findings indicated that the women higher in overall well being had notably more high involvement, high quality roles and fewer high involvement, low quality roles than the women lower in overall well-being.

Negoescu-Bodor, Olteanu and Popa (1990) conducted a comparative study on dimension of psycho-social adjustment in workers and longevous. The study was aimed to see difference in self-perception of health variable, activity levels and anxiety. The subjects were administered anxiety and depression scales and measures of activity and self perception of health. The analysis of discriminative data showed significant differences in self perception of health variable, activity levels and anxiety. These three variable accounted for 88 per cent of the 94 per cent variance.

Cedraschi and Merceron (1991) took a comparative analysis on Rorschach and Thematic Appreception Test (TAT) protocols of a young woman. An analysis was performed on the Roschach and Thematic Appreception Test (TAT) protocols of a young woman as false-self personality and a young man found typical of a pre-psychotic functioning with false self traits, Examiner-examinee relationship, narcissism, intellectualization and eroticization of the morbid were discussed as the salient features of study.

Harris and Brown (1992) carried out a study on selecting teaching as a profession. The objective of the study was to examine personality variables that may be salient in the selection and retension of those entering the teaching profession. The tools of the study such as Myers-Briggs Type Indicator and Locus of control scale were made and administered on the subjects in education field. The results indicated that those in education were more extroverted, preferred spontaniety and flexibility, and perceived their locus of reinforcement from close others.

Segal (1992) conducted a study on values personality and career choice among graduate social work female students and graduate business male students. The subjects were administered with California Psychological Inventory. The differences were correlated with the sex of the subjects. The results showed significant differences in the values and personalities of persons selecting professions with differing value bases.

Wong, Garfinkel and McLanshan (1993) conducted research on single mother families in eight countries. The sample included divorced, separated, widowed and never married women who were the heads of households and living with one or more children. The economic status of the single mothers was measured. The hypothesis was tested using multiple regression analysis. The results showed that economic status of single mothers in Canada and Australia did not differ very much from that of single mothers in the United States. It was also found that single mother families in all eight countries depended more or transfer income (both public and private than on earnings).

Fontana and Abouserie (1993) conducted a study to investigate whether individuals with certain personality characteristics experience significantly greater levels of teacher stress than do others. The objective was set to examine the relationship between stress level and personality traits among male and female teachers in primary and secondary schools. Professional Life Stress Scale (PLSS) and Eysenck Personality Questionnaire (EPG) were used as the tools of study. The results with regard to gender differences, the study revealed that there may be no very great variation between males and females in teacher stress. The other important finding of the study concerning the relationship between teacher's stress levels and personality state that there was a positive correlation between psychoticism (EPQP) and teacher stress. There was significant correlation between neuroticism (EPQN) and teacher stress.

The studies have shown that women higher in overall well being bear high involvement in high quality roles. The teachers are more extroverted and flexible in their nature. There exists significant differences in personal values and personality.

## 2.2 STUDIES CONDUCTED IN INDIA

### *(a)* Studies Related to Role Conflict

Singh (1972) carried out a study on the data from Punjab women to find out the motives for employment among working women and the relation between the motives for employment and Role Conflict. The study revealed that majority of women purely due to economic reason. It was also observed that the motives to seek employment and Role Conflict were closely related.

Bhoite (1973) carried out a study to analyse the roles of women employees who work under the developmental schemes as agents of social change. The sample was limited to the government and semi-government women employees in rural areas.

Intense Role Conflict was found in majority of the cases of those employed women. The study had noted down that the women employees suffered from various problems which arises out of rural environment.

Verma (1975) conducted a study on Role Conflict and the

corresponding role performance among head masters. The objectives of the study were to identify situations, which were perceived to be the Role Conflict situations and expectations. The main findings were that Role Conflict was positively related to worry. Role Conflict and sex were positively related. But Role Conflict and other institutional factors such as location, level, management of school were not significantly related. There was no existence of relationship between the Role Conflict and experience.

Rani (1976) examined the problem of Role Conflict among working women in Patna City. The objective of the study was set for employment. It was found that the main reason was the desire to make use of higher or professional education. Working due to gross economic necessity held the fourth rank in the measure of motivation. The correlation between motivation and occupation was found to be insignificant. Ill health, inflexible attitude of in-laws, unfriendly behaviour of friends and neighbourers and lack of positive support from the husband were found to be the main factor causing Role Conflict.

Dhillion (1981) conducted a study of Role Conflict among working women. The objectives of the study were to find out the nature and extent of Role Conflict faced by working women and to delineate the socio-economic factors affecting the Role Conflict. The study revealed the problem of Role Conflict in working women and identified the factor which helped or hindered the performance of home role and job role. A number of problems faced by working women were also observed which indirectly affected the performance of dual role.

Uma (1983) carried out a research project on social psychological study of women teachers to measure the relationship between the intensity of Role Conflict and need satisfaction of teachers. The next objective was framed to test the hypothesis that job Role Conflict is intense in a closed climate as compared to an open climate. The major findings of the study were that school teachers obtained a higher mean Role Conflict score, especially in home role situations as compared to college teachers. A significant mean differences existed between job security and need achievement among teachers who had worked for less than five years as compared to teachers with more than 5 years of experience.

Saita (1984) also studied Role Conflict among women teachers. Finding out of total Role Conflict, teaching role conflict and personality role conflict were taken as the objectives of the study. The major findings of the study were that there was a significant difference in the total Role Conflict experienced by women teachers. The results also supported that there was no significant difference in the social Role Conflict among women teachers working at different levels, *i.e.*, primary, secondary and at college level. The study also concluded that women teachers working at primary level felt more discipline Role Conflict than those working at secondary level.

Mane (1984) conducted research on women working in the Secretariat of Maharashtra Government. The study was aimed at identifying stresses and tensions under which women function in their dual roles as an earner and a home maker. Significant differences in the personal status and work situations of the women were found out. The respondents were adopted varied measures to contain the stress inherent in the situation and to cope with their dual role.

Mehta (1985) and Prasad (1985) also conducted their studies on Role Conflict among teachers. The major purposes of the study were to study the aspirations, adjustment and role conflict of school teachers. The studies concluded that the secondary school teachers and female teachers manifested higher educational aspiration than primary and male teachers respectively. Last but not the least finding of the study was that all groups of teachers suffered from role conflict but secondary school teachers scored significantly higher than primary school teachers on role conflict indices.

Rane (1986) and Sautha (1986) worked on increased psychological problems in society and changing role of mothers. The objective of the study was to examine the educational implications of the changing role of an Indian woman. The studies concluded that the main aspect of the problem of working mothers and their children was that the traditional role of the woman as a mother had not been changed inspite of her increased educational qualifications. The studies also revealed that education di not influence the attitude of women regarding their role in the cultural sphere.

Sinha (1988) conducted a study on a simple of 280 house-wives of Patna City. Women teachers constituted half of the sample for study. It was hypothesised that with respect to conflicting role and expectations, working wives will have more role conflicts than non-working wives. The results revealed that the working house-wives in general were more prone to role conflict than nonworking house-wives. On the basis of the results, it was concluded that working women have more family obligations and the extent of family obligations was positively related to role conflict.

Jindal (1990) studied conflict resolution behaviour and commitment to organization. A study of teachers perception in the colleges of Haryana was undertaken to find out organizational commitment in relation to experience, sex, location of colleges, nature of colleges etc. The teachers were administered conflict management inventory and organizational Commitment Questionnaire. The results concluded that women teacher had higher commitment in University colleges and private colleges in comparison to men teachers. Whereas men teachers had higher commitment in government colleges than women teachers. There was no significant correlation between commitment and teaching experience. Both male and female teachers had similar conflict resolution behaviour and commitment to organization.

The study concluded that role conflict and sex were positively related. But role conflict and location, management of school were not significantly related. Lack of emotional and financial support from near and dear were found to be the main factor causing role conflict. It was also supported that a teacher generally experiences role conflict on his or her way.

### (b) Studies Related to Working Conditions of Professional Women including Teachers

Sukhwal (1976) worked on attitudes of married lady teachers towards the teaching profession with the objective to investigate the felt problems in actual job situations in context of their dual role and to compare the professional attitudes of these women with their felt problems. Random sampling technique was choosen to select the appropriate sample. The felt problems in actual work conditions were identified with the help of a free projection test, the problem was categorised under four areas, that is, personal, financial, leave and timing, and educational. Women teachers wished to improve their service conditions, status and salaries.

Thakur (1978) studied working conditions of the married women teachers. The objectives were framed to know difficulties faced by them in their professional career and to evaluate their dual role as a wife and a mother. The data was collected with the help of the questionnaires and interview schedules. The findings of the study supported that they joined the teaching profession mainly for two reasons—economic and academic. It was also found that women teachers encountered many problems and difficulties in performing their role of a working wife.

Idrisi (1987) conducted a study of 200 teachers randomly selected from 13 institutions comprising of different grades keeping in view their representation from both sex as well as social belongingness. The tool used for the study was questionnaire prepared by Chauhan and Jain. The findings of the study supported that there was a significant difference in the level of teaching effectiveness between urban and rural areas. Rural teachers were found to be more effective than urban teachers. It was also found that female teachers were found to be more effective than the male teachers. There was no significant difference in the level of teaching effectiveness between high qualified teachers and low qualified teachers.

Mukhamath and Khadi (1991) conducted their studies on job satisfaction level among school teachers including female teachers. Data were collected through questionnaire regarding attitude towards teaching, family responsibility and income. The results showed that family responsibility and attitude towards teaching were the most influential factors for job involvement and satisfaction. Family responsibilities and job involvement were inversely related. Some teachers who had higher level of satisfaction were frustrated by feeling that they were underpaid and from being overly restricted by their supervisors.

It was observed that women teachers face a number of problems in their working conditions. These were academic, financial, personal, leave patterns and timings of their schools.

### (c) Studies Related to Personality and Allied Attributes of Professional Women including Teachers

Kaul (1972) conducted a factorial study of certain personality variables of popular teachers in secondary schools. The objectives of the study were to sort out the differentiating personality traits of popular teachers by studying the differences between the mean scores of popular and non popular teachers in the different traits of Cattell's 16 Personality Factors Questionnaire. It was found out that the popular teachers differentiated themselves on eleven personality traits of Cattell's 16 PF test. The popular teachers distinguished themselves as more outgoing, intelligent, emotionally stable, sober, conscientious, venturesome, tough-minded, shrewd, placid, controlled and relaxed. They were found to be low on economic and aesthetic values.

Shaheen (1973) conducted a sociological study of higher secondary school female teachers. The objectives of the study were to understand personal and social background of the respondents with a view to establish necessary association and correlation. And another purpose of the study was to enquire into the family size and its composition and to see its impact on the efficiency of women teachers. The findings regarding Socio-economic Status of teachers were dissatisfactory. The bulk of female teachers were from middle and lower socio-economic status.

Gautama (1974) carried out a sociometric study of the patterns of social interaction among principals, teachers and students in higher secondary schools of Himachal pradesh. The objective of the study was to study the patterns of social interaction and to have a comprehensive picture of patterns of social interaction in the school community. The study was restricted to rural and urban schools only. The tools employed were personality inventory by Saxena and Socio-economic Status by Kuppuswamy. The findings of the study revealed that patterns of social interaction found in the total sample. Tendencies of sex segregation and sex antagonism were found both among the teachers and the students, being more among the girl students as compared to boys. It was also found that there was a high positive association between the students socio-economic status and the positive social interaction amongst themselves.

Paranjapee (1974) conducted a study to explore the various socio-psychological problems that employed women graduates encounter in general and particularly in home adjustments, social and emotional adjustments, career orientation personality etc. The other objective of the study was to study the effects of marital status in different types of problems faced by the employed graduate ladies.

The study revealed that improved educational opportunities have raised women's qualification as well as their aspirations for participation in the economic world. The economic conditions had also made it imperative on the part of married and unmarried women particularly the educated ones to take up jobs.

Gupta (1978) carried out a study of secondary school teachers in Eastern Uttar Pradesh. The objectives of the study were to find out the overall status of secondary school teachers and to give some suggestions for the improvement in their status. The findings of the study were that the teachers working in rural areas commanded more social respect than those in urban areas. They were not satisfied in their present salary. They were provided suggestions to permit their teachers to take up tuitions for improving their economic status.

Gupta and Nisha (1978) carried out a study to find out personal factors affecting job satisfaction among secondary school teachers. Data were collected through questionnaires. An analysis of data revealed that job satisfaction was derived from and was caused by many interrelated factors. The highest correlation was found between age and job satisfaction. Furthermore, the importance of the various factors appeared to change from one situation to another.

Anand (1979) carried out a study to find out the relationship between job satisfaction and work role variables, and personality factors. It was found that fifty per cent of teachers working in schools were satisfied with their job in different schools of the Eastern States of India.

Gayatri (1980) framed a study on self concept of women teachers in different occupations to know self concept regarding their characteristics. The findings supported that female teachers were significantly more optimistic and more symbolic, intellectual and aesthetic. The study also revealed that the female teachers had significantly better self concept regarding their characteristics.

Porwal (1980) constructed a study on personality correlates of job satisfied higher secondary school teachers. The objectives of the study were to identify the personality traits and Socio-economic Status of the satisfied and dissatisfied teachers. The tools of the study were job satisfaction scale and 16 Personality Factors Questionnaire by Kapoor. The findings of the study supported that the satisfied teachers were more reserved, detached, critical, cool, stable, emotionally mature, faces reality, humble, mild, accommodating, trustworthy, retiring, adaptable, cautions, free from jealousy, practical, self assured, placid, socially precise, relaxed, unfrustrated and calm. On the other hand dissatisfied teachers were warm hearted, less stable, assertive, hard to fool. The study also concluded that female unmarried teachers were more satisfied.

Sharma (1981) studied mother child relationship as a

function of family size and socio-economic status among working housewives. The study was aimed to study the individual as well as collective impact of the family size and the Socio-economic Status on the eight dimensions of mother child relations among working class house-wives families. And also to study the factorial invariance of the eight dimensions that is acceptance-rejection, dominance-submission, encouragement-discouragement, love hate, trust-distrust, reward-punishment and tolerance-hostility in working class housewives families. The study was conducted as an ex-post facto. The study concluded a positive relationship between Socio-economic Status and eight dimensions of mother child relationship among working class housewives families. Working mothers with a moderate family size used punishment to maintain discipline.

Gupta (1981) conducted a comparative study of socio-economic problems and professional behaviour of men and women teachers in co-educational institutions at different levels in the state of Haryana. The objectives of the study were to compare the socio-economic background of male and female teachers to evaluate their basic environment. The randomly selected sample constituted of male and female teachers working in co-educational institutions. The teachers were administered the Kulshreshtha socio-economic status scale to evaluate the socio-economic status of the urban as well as rural teachers. The study concluded that the socio-economic status of the teachers at primary, middle, secondary and college levels were more or less similar. Female school teachers were more democratic, indirect and gave encouraging statements in the class room than the male counterparts.

Kakkar (1983) undertook a research project on job satisfaction in relation to attitudes, job values and vocational interests of women. The study investigated the impact of vocational attitudes, interests and work values on the job satisfaction of women employees who had entered the world of work after initial vocational training. The variables of the study were socio-economic status, marital status, age, work values as independent variables and job satisfaction as a dependent variable. The study also revealed positive relationships between job satisfaction and occupation level, job satisfaction and age, educational level, income, vocational attitude, work values.

Som (1984) conducted a study on teachers' personality pattern and their attitudes towards teaching and related areas. The main objective of the study was to find out the descriptive personality pattern of teachers with reference to the dimension of extraversion-introversion and the traits involved there. Another purpose of the study was to observe the relative importance of the extraversion variables in the determination of the teachers' attitude towards teaching-profession, teaching, class room teaching and pupils. The major findings concluded that the secondary school teachers were neither extrovert nor introvert and they could be tentatively described as lacking patience but possessing soberiety, carefulness, temporal thought, introspection, concentration and mental exertion in terms of extroversion-introversion traits. Female teachers were found to be higher than male teachers in their attitudes towards teaching, teaching profession, classroom teaching and pupils.

Mishra (1987) studied the influence of occupational stress and job satisfaction on involvement of a random sample of 400 railway employees in India. It was hypothesized that there would be significant differences between mean job involvement scores of (1) high and low occupational stress groups, and (2) high and low job satisfaction groups. The study showed the results that job-involvement scores were related only to job satisfaction. Occupational stress and job satisfaction had a significant negative relationship.

Kumar (1991) conducted a study on teacher effectiveness among different groups of teachers in relation with personality traits. The objectives of the study were to determine personality traits among different groups of teachers and also to determine relationship between teacher effectiveness and personality traits among different groups. The design of the study was ex-post facto. Teacher effectiveness scale by Kumar and Mutha was used to measure teacher effectiveness. Second, the Sixteen Personality Factors Questionnaire was used to determine personality traits. The findings of the study were that teacher effectiveness and personality traits of Arts teachers had no relationship. Teacher effectiveness and personality traits of Commerce teachers have negative relationship. Teacher effectiveness and personality traits of Science teachers have no relationship.

Tiwari (1992) designed the study to highlight the perceptions of working and non-working women. The sample consisted of 60 females and included six different categories. Affective, status related, ability related, habit related, personality and social characteristics which were rated on a seven point scale. The findings supported the hypothesis that working women, non-working women and college going girls did not differ in their perceptions of working and non-working women. It was concluded that all women were equal whether working or non-working.

The study reported that female teachers faced socio-psychological problems on their way. The socio-economic status was found to be dissatisfactory. Some of the studies observed positive relationship of socio-economic status with job satisfaction. Other studies have shown that teacher effectiveness and personality factors bear negative relationship. The study also reported that there existed a positive relationship between socio-economic status among working wives. Socio-economic status of the teachers at (primary, middle, secondary and college) all levels were more or less similar. Female teachers were found to be more democratic and indirect than the male teachers.

## 2.3 PRESENT STUDY IN RELATION TO THE LITERATURE REVIEWED

After reviewing the studies conducted in India and abroad, the researcher concluded that role conflict among women teachers is comparatively an ignored area in educational research. However, there are some studies related to role conflict among working women and industrial workers.

Almost all the researchers have done very little to unfold the obscurities of role conflict and to know various variables related to it. There are varied findings with some contradictions and it is difficult to generalize them to contribute to the development of a role conflict theory. For instance, some of the research abstracts and research reports support that role stress, role ambiguity, multiple roles, work demands, incompatible roles are the terms similar to role conflict while other researches support that role conflict, role ambiguity, quantitative overload and quantitative underload are the varying forms of role stress.

The review of the related literature in a nutshell has revealed the following important aspects about role conflict :

1. Working women experience high Role Conflict.
2. Sex of the subject is significantly related to the role conflict. Females experience more role conflict.
3. Personality is related to role conflict more in the case of women as compared to their male counterparts.
4. In some studies, no discrimination was followed on the basis of sex regarding traditional sex roles.
5. No study was carried out on role conflict among women teachers in Haryana schools.
6. Some of the researchers related the socio-economic status (SES) to role conflict among working women.
7. No study was conducted and concluded that women are burdened thrice *i.e.* in family role, job role and social role. Social role was never studied along with dual role conflict.
8. No study had discriminated between inter role conflict and intra role conflict respectively.
9. There is no justification in the argument that working women are different from non-working women.
10. No research was undertaken regarding Inter Family Role Conflict (FRCI) Inter Job Role Conflict (JRCI) and Intra-family Role Conflict (FRCI) Intra-job Role Conflict (JRCI).

It is found that there are a number of researches regarding students, their personality achievement, socio-economic status and other aspects of educational administration and management. The number of researches on teachers, women teachers and other variables related to teachers is meagre. Therefore, the researcher undertook this study on Role Conflict among women teachers. The present survey of related literature has been definitely useful in framing the hypotheses and designing the study which appear in the following chapters. The investigator made an humble attempt to fill up the described gaps by undertaking the present study.

# 3 Plan and Procedure

Collection of data constitutes important pre-requisites in conducting research study but for which it becomes difficult to complete the work. In this context, Mouley (1964) remarked, "Scientific problems can be solved only on the basis of data and a major responsibility of the scientists is to set up a research design capable of providing data necessary to the solution of the problem. While the unity of research makes it possible to say that one aspect is more crucial than another, the collection of data is of paramount importance, in conducting research since obviously, no selection can be more adequate than the data on which it is based".

For the collection of data, the investigator has to set up the design, specify the sampling method, the nature of population and sample, the tools used for the collection of data, their tabulation and organisation and the statistical techniques used.

The present research aims at studying women teachers experiencing role conflict while performing different roles like family role, job role, and social role. To find out the nature and extent of role conflict J.B.T. and B. Ed. women teachers were selected for this study. The detailed procedure has been given in the lines to follow.

## 3.1 RESEARCH METHODOLOGY

The decision about the methods to be employed for accomplishment of aims and objectives of research depends upon the nature of the problem selected and the kind of data necessary. In practice, the following methods have been accepted in the field of educational research.

*(i)* Historical research describes what was. The process involves investigating, analysing and interpreting. The events of the past for the purpose of discovering generalization that are helpful in understanding the past and the present, and, to a limited extent in anticipating the future.

*(ii)* Experimental research describes what will be when certain variables are carefully controlled or manipulated. The focus is on variable relationship as defined here, deliberate manipulation is always a part of the experimental methods.

*(iii)* Descriptive research describes what is, describing, recording, analysing and interpreting conditions that exist. It involves some type of comparison or contrast and attempts to discover relationships between manipulated variables.

The choice of the methods depends on the purpose of the study because more significant differences also exist with respect to the purpose which the method is to serve, the nature of the problem for which they are appropriate and the procedure employed in the conduct of each.

The present methodology of this study is based on descriptive research. Best and Kahn (1989) state that "descriptive research is concerned with all of the following : hypothesis formulation and testing, the analysis of the relationships between non manipulated variables and the development of generalization—in descriptive research variables that exist or have already occurred are selected and observed.

As is evident from the definition, descriptive research not only concerns itself with formulations and testing of hypotheses but also analysing the relationships existing between various variables. The stress is also laid on the generalizations developed from the piece of research. Thus, the descriptive method was considered most appropriate for conducting the study of women teachers. In this study, role conflict of women teachers was taken as dependent variable and personality factors, and some demographic variables including socio-economic status were taken as independent variables.

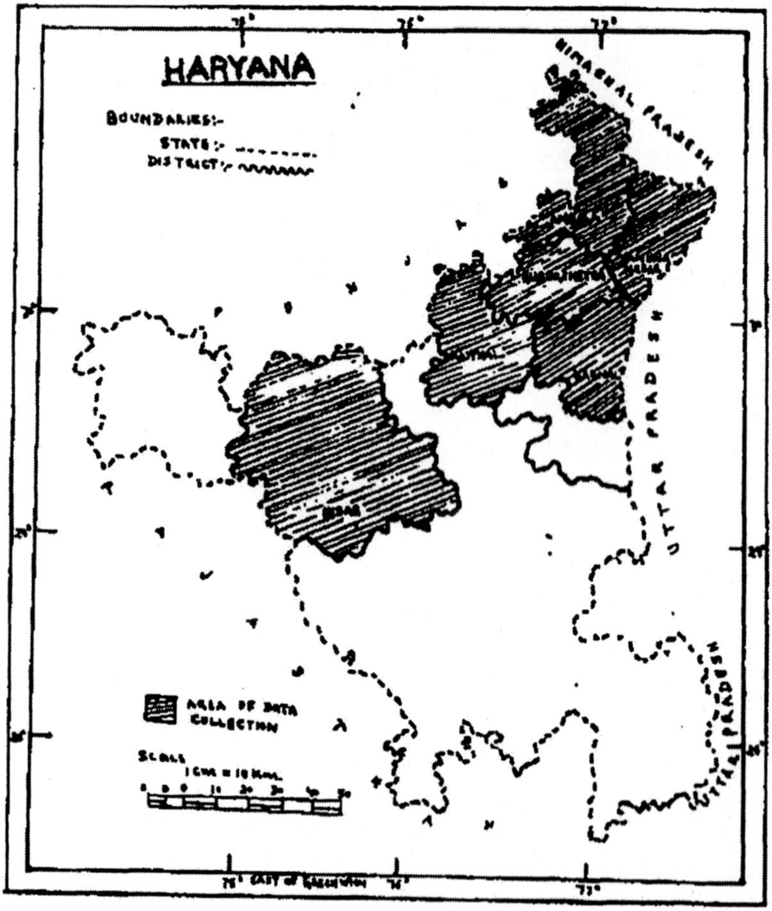


Fig. 3.1

The method and technique used to pick up the appropriate population and sample is given in the next lines.

## 3.2 POPULATION AND SAMPLE

The main purpose of research is to discover principles that have universal application, but to study a whole population to arrive at generalization would be impracticable, if not impossible. At times, some populations are so large that their characteristics cannot be measured, before the measurement could be completed, the population would have changed.

During recent years sampling has been increasingly used in education to ascertain information necessary in responding certain questions about a specific population. Since it has been reported that even if a small representative sample can be drawn from the entire population, than the parameters are easily represented and estimated by the sample statistics. In this context, it is important to know that the collection has to be restricted to a sample which becomes representative of the whole.

The women teachers working in various schools in the state of Haryana constituted population for the present study. But it was difficult to include all of them in the purview of this work keeping in mind time, physical and financial constraints. That is why it was decided to select a small proportion of them for the sake of conducting this research study.

### 3.3 SIZE AND SAMPLE

As already reported the state of Haryana comprised area of the study. For the sake of administrative convenience, Haryana has been divided into 16 districts. Out of these, 6 districts were randomly selected for the purview of this work. These districts were Hisar, Kurukshetra, Karnal, Kaithal, Yamuna Nagar and Ambala. The investigator procured a list of all the primary and secondary schools from the offices of the respective District Education Officers and randomly selected a total number of 75 schools from all the above stated six districts. While selecting these schools, only Government, private and aided schools were considered—public schools and convent schools were excluded from this study. However, the schools situated in urban areas and rural areas were also considered. Thus, as many as 360 women teachers (an equal number of women teachers working in rural and urban areas, *i.e.* 180 each) randomly picked up from boys, girls and co-educational schools constituted the sample.

**Table 3.1 District-wise Distribution of the Sample**

| *Sr. No.* | *Name of the District* | *No. of Schools* | *No. of Women Teachers* |
|---|---|---|---|
| 1. | Hisar | 18 | 120 |
| 2. | Kurukshetra | 18 | 120 |
| 3. | Karnal | 10 | 50 |
| 4. | Ambala | 10 | 25 |
| 5. | Yamuna Nagar | 9 | 25 |
| 6. | Kaithal | 10 | 20 |
| | Grand Total | 75 | 360 |

## 3.4 TOOLS USED

For data collection, a variety of devices may be used keeping in view the suitability of the study. Therefore, selection of appropriate tools is of vital importance for collection of data which depends on various considerations such as objectives of the study, availability of suitable tests and scales, personal competence of the investigator to administer, score and interpret the results.

As this study is focussed upon the socio-psychological correlates of role conflict in women teachers, the investigator selected the following tools for the present study :

3.4.1 Role Conflict Scale for women teachers prepared by the investigator herself.

3.4.2 Socio-economic Status scale by R. Bhardwaj, S. Gupta, and N.S. Chauhan.

3.4.3 16 Personality Factors Questionnaire (Form A) by R.B. Cattell and H.W. Eber.

### 3.4.1 Role Conflict Scale for Women Teachers

This scale is intended to measure the extent of role conflict in women teachers. It was constructed and standardized by the investigator herself. Role conflict is categorised into two broad heads *i.e.* Inter-Role Conflict and Intra-Role Conflict. The Scale provides separate measures of Role Conflict into following areas :

I. Inter-Role Conflict
   (a) Family role
   (b) Job role, and
   (c) Social role

II. Intra-Role Conflict
   (a) Family role
   (b) Job role and
   (c) Social role

III. Dual role *i.e.* family role as well as job role.

In all, there are 46 items which are widely distributed into respective areas of role conflict. The respondents are required to record their responses into 5 categories *i.e.* always, often, occasionally, seldom and never. The scale is non-timed *i.e.* there is no specified time limit to complete the scale. Generally, the subject takes about 30 to 35 minutes to record her responses.

### *(a)* Reliability of the Role Conflict Scale

The reliability of the scale was found by split-half method. And it was found to be .85 alongwith areawise reliability.

**Table 3.2 Split-half Reliability Co-efficients of Role Conflict Scale for Women Teachers**

| *Sr. No.* | *Role Conflict Areas* | $r_{tt}$ |
|---|---|---|
| 1. | Inter Role Conflict | .72 |
| 2. | Intra-Role Conflict | .66 |
| 3. | Family Role Conflict | .64 |
| 4. | Job Role Conflict | .67 |
| 5. | Social Role Conflict | .60 |
| 6. | Dual Role Conflict | .90 |
| 7. | Role Conflict Scale (As a whole) | .85 |

### *(b)* Validity of Role Conflict Scale

Experts opinion were obtained to establish the face validity and content validity. Concurrent validity was also established against the criterion of Teachers' Role Conflict inventory by Prasad and Bhushan (TRCI) on the same sample. It was found to be 0.97.

### 3.4.2 Cattell's 16 Personality Factors Questionnaire : A Brief Description

The Sixteen Personality Factors Questionnaire (16 PF) is developed by basic research in psychology to give almost a complete coverage of personality. The test was designed for use with individuals aged sixteen and above. This test is available in six Forms : A, B, C, D, E and F. Forms A, B, C and D are most appropriate for literates and E, F are designed for individuals with marked educational and reading difficulties.

Cattell's Sixteen Personality Factors Questionnaire was selected because of the following reasons :

*(a)* The '16 PF' Questionnaire is an objectively scorable test devised by basic research in psychology to give the most complete coverage of personality possible in a brief time.

*(b)* Coverage of personality by this test is ensured by the sixteen functionally independent and psychologically meaningful dimensions isolated by over twenty years of factor analytic research on normal and clinical groups.

*(c)* Factors measured by the '16 PF' Questionnaire are not just peculiar to this test. They have been established as unitary, psychologically meaningful entities in many researches in various life situations. To quote Vernon, "Cattell's basic personality factors were extracted from LR data, provided by successively reducing the complete list of personality trait—names given by Allport and Odbert. By this method he hoped to

ensure comprehensive coverage of the whole sphere of personality."

*(d)* The sixteen dimensions or scales of '16 PF' Questionnaire are independent, that is the correlation between one and another is found to be quite small. Therefore, having a certain position on one does not prevent the person's having any position whatever on any other. Thus, each of the sixteen scales brings an entirely new piece of information about the person, a condition not found in many alleged multi-dimensional scales.

For the present study, Form A of the test was used. This test generally requires about 45 to 60 minutes for administration. There are 187 Questions in Form A. There are ten to thirteen Questions for each factor (trait). The questions are arranged in a roughly cyclic order determined by a plan to give maximum convenience in scoring by stencil and to ensure variety and interest for the examinee. Three alternative answers are provided for each of the question. The answers are to be recorded on separate answer sheet.

For convenience, these dimensions are set out briefly as below. Each factor is listed with its alphabetic designation and brief description of low and high scores.

**Table 3.3 Description of 16 Personality Factors**

| *Factor* | *Low Sten Score (1-3)* | *High Sten Score (8-10)* |
|---|---|---|
| *1* | *2* | *3* |
| A | Reserved, detached, Critical aloof, stiff | Outgoing, warm hearted, easy going, participating |
| B | Dull | Bright |
| C | Affected by feelings, emotionally less table easily upset, changeable | Emotionally stable, mature faces reality, calm |

*(Contd.)*

*(Contd.)*

| *1* | *2* | *3* |
|---|---|---|
| E | Humble, mild, easily led docile, accommodating | Assertive, aggressive, competitive, stubborn |
| F | Sober, taciturn, serious | Happy go luckly, enthusiastic |
| G | Expedient, disregards rules | Conscientious, persistent moralistic, staid |
| H | Shy, timid, threat-sensitive | Venturesome, uninhibited, socially bold |
| I | Tough-minded, self reliant, realistic | Tender minded, sensitive, clinging, overprotected |
| L | Trusting, accepting conditions | Suspicious, hard to fool |
| M | Practical, "down-to-earth" concerns | Imaginative, absent-minded bohemian |
| N | Forthright, unpretentious genuine but socially clumsy | Astute, polished, socially aware |
| O | Self assured, placid, secure, complacent | Apprehensive, self-reproaching, insecure, worrying, troubled |
| $Q_1$ | Conservative, respecting traditional ideas | Experimenting, liberal free thinking |
| $Q_2$ | Group dependent, a "joiner" and sound follower | Self-sufficient, resourceful, prefer own decisions |
| $Q_3$ | Undisciplined self-conflict, lax, follows own urges, careless of social rules | Controlled exacting will power, socially precise, compulsive, following self-image |
| $Q_4$ | Relaxed, tranquill, torpid, unfrustrated composed | Tense, frustrated, driven, overwrought |

**(*a*) Consistencies of 16 PF Questionnaire**

The consistencies of 16 PF scale are given as below :

**Table 3.4. Consistencies of 16 PF Scale**

| Form | *16 PF Dependability Coefficients : Test-Retest tih 2 to 7 day interval*<br><br>*N = 146 American subjects* | *16 PF Stability Coefficients : Test-Retest with 2 to 48 months intervals*<br><br>*N = 44* | *Equivalence Coefficient of test forms for each trait Form A with B*<br><br>*N = 6476* |
|---|---|---|---|
| | For Form A | | |
| Factors | | | |
| A | .81 | .80 | .57 |
| B | .58 | .43 | .49 |
| C | .78 | .66 | .54 |
| E | .80 | .65 | .52 |
| F | .79 | .74 | .61 |
| G | .81 | .49 | .47 |
| H | .83 | .80 | .71 |
| I | .77 | .85 | .59 |
| L | .75 | .75 | .37 |
| M | .70 | .35 | .40 |
| N | .61 | .35 | .21 |
| O | .79 | .70 | .59 |
| $Q_1$ | .73 | .50 | .34 |
| $Q_2$ | .73 | .57 | .39 |
| $Q_3$ | .62 | .36 | .43 |
| $Q_4$ | .81 | .66 | .62 |

**(b) Validity**

The validity of the test itself is meant to be a concept (or "Construct") validity. That is to say, the test questions (or items), as stated above, are chosen as being good measures of the personality factors, as these factors as represented in research analysis.

**Table 3.5. Direct Concept Validities of the 16 PF Scale**

| Form | A | B | C | E | F | G | H | I | L |
|---|---|---|---|---|---|---|---|---|---|
| | .79 | .35 | .70 | .63 | .83 | .67 | .92 | .70 | .49 |
| | M | N | O | $Q_1$ | $Q_2$ | $Q_3$ | $Q_4$ | | |
| | .44 | .41 | .71 | .62 | .70 | .68 | .57 | | |

### 3.4.5 Socio-Economic Status Scale by R. Bhardwaj S. Gupta & N.S. Chauhan

The present scale of Socio economic Status has been developed for literate people. It can be administered on illiterate people for personal interviews. The scale gives three-rank-values *i.e.* area rank value, item rank value, and alternative rank value. With the help of these three rank values the proportion rank sale value is calculated and then weighted scores for each item is determined.

The Socio-economic Status Scale provides weighted scores area-wise for father, mother and self *i.e.* subjects. The seven areas of measures are given as below : *(a)* Family, *(b)* Social, *(c)* Education, *(d)* Profession, *(e)* Caste, *(f)* Total assets, and *(g)* Monthly income.

There is no time limit for the subject to record the responses in this scale. Ordinarily an individual takes about 10 to 15 minutes to record her responses.

#### (*a*) Reliability of the Socio-Economic Status Scale

The reliability of the test was found by test-retest method and it was found in seven areas and of the scale as a whole.

**Table 3.6. Reliability Coefficients of Socio-economic Status Scale**

| *Sr. No.* | *Areas* | *Coefficients of Correlation* |
|---|---|---|
| 1. | Family | .72 |
| 2. | Social | .68 |
| 3. | Education | .82 |
| 4. | Profession | .76 |
| 5. | Caste | .92 |
| 6. | Total assets | .67 |
| 7. | Monthly income | .73 |
| | Scale as a whole | .75 |

### (b) Validity of the Socio-Economic Status Scale

The content validity of the scale was solely based on research proven items and was expected to be high and promising.

## 3.5 ADMINISTRATION OF THE QUESTIONNAIRES

All the Questionnaires namely—Role Conflict Scale, Personality factors questionnaire and socio-economic status scale were administered individually. Before administration the subject was made aware that the test was meant for research work only and the responses would be kept confidential. Therefore, the subject was requested to be free, frank, honest and sincere in answering the test items.

Then all these three tools mentioned under preceded headings were administered one by one. However, the tests can be virtually self-administering but to establish good rapport, the investigator gave the instructions to the women teachers. In the end, the woman teacher was asked to clear the doubts if she had any.

The tests were untimed, but generally the subjects took 1½ to 2 hours for the completion of tests. Then the investigator made sure that all the questions had been responded and only single answer for each question was given by the respondent.

## 3.6 SCORING

The scoring was done as per the instructions of each questionnaire/scale as given below :

### (a) Scoring Pattern of Role Conflict Scale

The scoring of the scale is very easy and quantitative type. Scoring provides the weightage score for each item. The responses of the subjects were rated on a five point scale ranging from always, often, occasionally, seldom, and never. The scoring is done by awarding 5 scores to "always", 4 to "often", 3 to "occasionally" 2 to "seldom" and 1 to "never" for negative statements, and *vice-versa* for positive statements respectively.

The scoring procedure has been clearly illustrated in the following able :

**Table 3.7. Scoring Procedure of Role Conflict Scale**

| *Sr.No.* | *No. of Alternatives* | *Positive Statement* | *Negative Statement* |
|---|---|---|---|
| 1. | Always | 1 | 5 |
| 2. | Often | 2 | 4 |
| 3. | Occasionally | 3 | 3 |
| 4. | Seldom | 4 | 2 |
| 5. | Never | 5 | 1 |

### *(b)* Scoring of 16 PF Questionnaire

Answer sheets of 16 PF (Form A) thus collected were scored with the help of two cardboard stencil scoring keys. One key covers the factors (traits) : A, C, F, H, L, N, $Q_1$ and $Q_3$ and the other key, factors : B, E, G, I, M, O, $Q_2$ and $Q_4$. Each answer scores 0, 1 and 2 points except the trait B answers which was scored 0 for incorrect and score 1 for correct answer. The total score for each of the sixteen traits was recorded on the specified space of the answer sheet. Thus separate scores were obtained for each student for all the sixteen factors. These were then converted into sten scores.

### *(c)* Scoring of Socio-Economic Status Scale

Scoring of the scale was of a quantitative type. Scoring key provided the weightage score for each item. Every alternative of each item has only one weighted score in the horizontal plane for father, mother and the subjects. The scoring key was placed vertically between two assigned points on the test. The separate scores for each area were totalledvertically. These totals of the scores for each separate area were put in big boxes provided at the vertical end of each area for father, mother and the case.

Each page of the scale was scored by the same process. But separate scoring keys were used for each page of the test. The minimum and maximum scores may range between 39 to 70 respectively.

## 3.7 CLASSIFICATION OF THE DATA

The data thus collected for testing the hypotheses were

classified on the basis of the following demographic variables :

*(a)* Educational level in terms of J.B.T. and B.Ed.

*(b)* Marital Status in terms of married and unmarried.

*(c)* Location of the School, *i.e.* rural and urban.

*(d)* Type of family *i.e.* nuclear and joint.

*(e)* Teaching experience *i.e.* more than 5 years and less than 5 years, and

*(f)* Management of the school *i.e.* Government, aided and private

*(g)* Type of school *i.e.* girls, boys and co-educational.

## 3.8 STATISTICAL TECHNIQUES USED

The following techniques were used for analysis of the data :

1. K-S Test was employed to study the nature of distribution of Role Conflict Scores among women teachers.
2. Mean, median or $P_{50}$ or ($Q_2$), $P_{75}$ or ($Q_3$), $P_{25}$ or ($Q_1$), were determined to find out the nature and incidence of role conflict among women teachers.
3. Product Moment coefficient of correlation was employed to find out the socio-psychological correlates of role conflict among women teachers.
4. "t" Test was used to find out the significance of difference between mean scores of role conflict with respect to demographic variables.

# 4 Construction and Standardization of Role Conflict Scale

The term Role Conflict has been used by various sociologists and social psychologists to indicate the problem-situations which arise due to incompatible roles. Sarbin (1954) states that role conflicts "occur when a person occupies two or more positions simultaneously and when the role expectations of one are incompatible with the role expectations of the others." Similarly Goode (1960 views that the role strain or role stress (West Woode, 1967) can be used in the same sense as role conflict. The basic component behind the phenomenon is inconsistency of roles.

A woman teacher has to play a number of role to meet the responsibilities, expectations and different demands, needs of family members and society. By doing so, she often suffers from the problem of role conflict/stress due to conflicting nature of expectations of others. A number of studies have shown that role conflict is associated with variations in spouse support, less job satisfaction, increased household responsibilities, meagre pay, more demands, problem of child-care and worse working conditions. (Halehan and Gilbert 1979), (Sukhwal, 1976), (Singh 1981).

The findings of Som (1984) based on the study of teachers' personality patterns and their attitudes towards teaching and related areas established that female teachers were found to be higher than male teachers in their attitudes toward teaching, teaching profession, classroom teaching and pupils.

These studies reveal that a woman teacher meet the problematic situation under three conflicting areas in relation to her family, school and society.

## 4.1 INTER ROLE CONFLICT AND INTRA ROLE CONFLICT

Role Conflict is defined as the situation in which an individual is expected to play two or more different roles that involve responses and are antagonistic in nature and thus, cause role conflict.

The investigator also tried to study role conflict into two distinct categories *i.e.* inter role conflict and intra role conflict. Each of the categories included family role, job role, and social role, dual role. These two categories of role conflict has been studied by Deutch (1969), Gatzals and Guba (1955), Sarbin (1954), *et al.*, *i.e.* inter role conflict takes place when a person occupies two or more positions simultaneously and meet to incompatible role expectations of others and intra role conflict arises from a number of sources within a specific role.

It was in this direction that the need of a development of role conflict scale is felt to delineate the picture of role conflict as no scale is available to measure role conflict among women teachers. No doubt Parsad and Bhusan (1991) constructed and standardised a Teachers' Role Conflict Inventory (TRCI) which meant for teachers in general but it was not applicable for women teachers in particular.

Planning of the scale is the first step in any type of scale construction. In the planning of the scale, generally the purpose of the scale, content of the scale, medium and type of the scale, items and instructions for whom the scale was made in the population were to be kept in mind. The procedure of development and standardization of this scale was carried out through the following steps :

—Preparation of first draft

—Reliability; and

—Validity.

## 4.2 PREPARATION OF FIRST DRAFT

A blue print of the scale was prepared which after passing through the stages mentioned underneath, formed the first draft of the scale. These stages were item formulation, item selection, item difficulty, item analysis and item validity. The description of these stages has been given in the proceeding lines :

**(a) Item Formulation**

The statements were formulated from different sources *i.e.* relevant literature, interview with female teachers, discussion with research scholars working in the field of women studies, and delebrations held with the experts in the field of psychology and sociology. All these statements were framed so as to assess the problem of role conflict among women teachers at school level. In this way, 65 statements were framed.

**(b) Item Selection**

The list of statements so prepared, was reviewed. First of all, the items were judged from language point of view. The statements which were having ambiguity, were either modified or dropped out. After this, the list of these statements were given to the panel of ten judges. These judges consulted and comprised female teachers from various University Teaching Departments. They were requested to point out duplication or overlapping items with some suggestions. After this, the scale was administered to a small group of women teachers of different schools to know whether these statements were properly followed by them or not. The statements which were not properly interpreted or followed, were either dropped out or modified.

In this way, only 60 statements were retained in the preliminary draft *i.e.* 27 statements were comprised in inter role conflict, 31 statements included in intra role conflict and two in common way.

**(c) Administration of the Preliminary Draft**

It was administered individually on 100 women teachers in the schools. The instructions were explained to the respondents. They were asked to tick either of the five answer appearing in the five point scale. There was no time limit for completing the scale. Generally a teacher completed the scale within 35 minutes.

### *(d)* Scoring

The scoring of the scale is very easy and quantitative type. Scoring key provides the weightage score for each item. The responses of the subject were rated on a five point scale ranging from Always, Often, Occasionally, Seldom and Never. The scoring is done by awarding 5 scores to "always", 4 to "Often", 3 to "Occasionally" 2 to "Seldom" and 1 to "Never" for negative statements and *vice versa* for positive statements respectively.

The scoring procedure has been clearly illustrated in the following table.

**Table 4.1. Scoring Procedure of Role Conflict Scale**

| *Sr.No.* | *No. of Alternatives* | *Positive Statement* | *Negative Statement* |
|---|---|---|---|
| 1. | Always | 1 | 5 |
| 2. | Often | 2 | 4 |
| 3. | Occasionally | 3 | 3 |
| 4. | Seldom | 4 | 2 |
| 5. | Never | 5 | 1 |

### *(e)* Item Analysis

After answer scripts have been scored, item analysis was done. Item analysis is primarily concerned with item difficulty and item discrimination. Item difficulty is taken in terms of proportion of individuals completing the items successfully but here, there is no pass or fail on any item. So indices of item difficulty can not be determined.

Item discrimination index refers to the degree to which it differentiates between those obtaining high and low scores. All the scores of each item were arranged in ascending order of total scores. The top 27 per cent and the bottom 27 per cent scripts were taken out. The significance of the difference between the mean scores in each item the top and bottom piles were tested. The items which showed a significant difference in favour of the upper group were considered to be worth retaining.

The formula used for 't' test is as follows :

$N_1 = N_2$

$$t = \frac{M_1 - M_2}{SE_D}$$

or

$$t = \frac{M_1 - M_2}{\sqrt{\frac{\sigma_1}{N_1 - 1} + \frac{\sigma_2}{N_2 - 1}}}$$

When $M_1$ = Mean of the upper 27% of the cases

$M_2$ = Mean of the lower 27% of the cases

$\sigma_1$ = SD of the upper group

$\sigma_2$ = SD of the lower group

$N_1 - 1$ = frequency of the upper group

$N_2 - 1$ = frequency of the lower group

Values of t were judged at .05 and .01 level of significance.

The results of item analysis are given in Table 4.2.

**Table 4.2. Difference Between Mean Scores of Women Teachers**

| *Sr. No. (Items)* | *Higher Group* | | *Lower Group* | | *'t'* |
|---|---|---|---|---|---|
| | *($M_1$) Mean* | *($\sigma_1$) S.D.$_1$* | *($M_2$) Mean* | *($\sigma_2$) S.D.$_2$* | |
| *1* | *2* | *3* | *4* | *5* | *6* |
| 1. | 4.66 | 0.556 | 3.74 | 2.237 | 2.960 |
| 2. | 4.51 | 1.771 | 2.07 | 1.698 | 7.109 |
| 3. | 3.11 | 1.212 | 1.55 | 1.535 | 5.200 |
| 4. | 3.11 | 1.599 | 1.33 | 0.720 | 5.390 |
| 5. | 1.59 | 0.913 | 1.51 | 0.827 | 0.327* |
| 6. | 3.51 | 1.084 | 3.00 | 1.305 | 1.700* |
| 7. | 2.74 | 1.264 | 2.14 | 1.267 | 2.127 |
| 8. | 3.00 | 1.563 | 2.29 | 1.628 | 2.052 |

*(Contd.)*

*(Contd.)*

| *1* | *2* | *3* | *4* | *5* | *6* |
|---|---|---|---|---|---|
| 9. | 1.96 | 0.737 | 1.33 | 0.816 | 2.837 |
| 10. | 3.59 | 0.234 | 2.66 | 1.622 | 3.811 |
| 11. | 3.40 | 1.851 | 1.74 | 1.074 | 5.030 |
| 12. | 2.14 | 1.177 | 1.07 | 0.377 | 2.152 |
| 13. | 4.22 | 0.737 | 1.66 | 0.942 | 11.342 |
| 14. | 3.62 | 0.928 | 1.37 | 0.867 | 9.221 |
| 15. | 1.77 | 1.342 | 2.88 | 1.382 | 3.512 |
| 16. | 2.00 | 1.138 | 1.14 | 0.755 | 3.520 |
| 17. | 2.85 | 1.483 | 1.00 | 0.000 | 8.295 |
| 18. | 2.03 | 1.137 | 1.11 | 0.566 | 4.107 |
| 19. | 3.14 | 1.788 | 3.25 | 1.897 | 0.305 |
| 20. | 1.81 | 1.155 | 1.03 | 0.195 | 3.611 |
| 21. | 2.77 | 0.895 | 1.11 | 0.855 | 6.803 |
| 22. | 4.07 | 1.288 | 2.59 | 1.533 | 5.033 |
| 23. | 3.18 | 1.441 | 2.00 | 1.414 | 3.806 |
| 24. | 3.11 | 1.286 | 1.22 | 0.496 | 8.475 |
| 25. | 3.74 | 1.157 | 1.81 | 0.862 | 7.310 |
| 26. | 2.96 | 1.690 | 2.33 | 1.296 | 2.032 |
| 27. | 2.96 | 1.559 | 2.74 | 1.235 | 0.733* |
| 28. | 3.29 | 1.771 | 2.77 | 1.812 | 1.502* |
| 29. | 2.48 | 1.123 | 2.44 | 1.342 | 1.330* |
| 30. | 4.18 | 1.396 | 3.18 | 1.564 | 3.030 |
| 31. | 3.88 | 0.942 | 1.37 | 0.823 | 6.188 |
| 32. | 1.66 | 1.346 | 3.40 | 1.638 | 5.272 |
| 33. | 3.03 | 1.805 | 2.59 | 2.468 | 1.631* |
| 34. | 3.33 | 2.341 | 2.14 | 1.648 | 3.131 |
| 35. | 2.66 | 1.247 | 3.00 | 1.598 | 5.320 |
| 36. | 3.33 | 0.785 | 1.00 | 0.000 | 13.705 |

*(Contd.)*

*(Contd.)*

| *1* | *2* | *3* | *4* | *5* | *6* |
|---|---|---|---|---|---|
| 37. | 2.11 | 1.358 | 1.29 | 0.760 | 3.106 |
| 38. | 1.92 | 1.423 | 2.03 | 1.400 | 0.348* |
| 39. | 3.48 | 1.314 | 1.00 | 0.000 | 11.272 |
| 40. | 2.44 | 1.257 | 1.07 | 0.282 | 6.227 |
| 41. | 1.88 | 1.210 | 1.33 | 0.471 | 2.500 |
| 42. | 1.70 | 1.250 | 3.55 | 1.422 | 6.160 |
| 43. | 2.22 | 1.330 | 1.59 | 1.162 | 2.100 |
| 44. | 2.03 | 0.701 | 1.03 | 0.269 | 5.882 |
| 45. | 1.37 | 0.583 | 1.18 | 0 395 | 1.117* |
| 46. | 1.25 | 0.626 | 1.03 | 0.269 | 1.941 |
| 47. | 2.29 | 0.737 | 1.77 | 1.314 | 1.969 |
| 48. | 2.88 | 1.974 | 1.29 | 0.710 | 3.633 |
| 49. | 3.74 | 1.547 | 1.00 | 0.00 | 12.454 |
| 50. | 2.55 | 1.806 | 1.07 | 0.282 | 5.606 |
| 51. | 1.74 | 1.321 | 1.18 | 0.269 | 6.393 |
| 52. | 2.14 | 1.296 | 1.40 | 0.871 | 2.803 |
| 53. | 3.00 | 1.414 | 2.40 | 1.194 | 2.000 |
| 54. | 3.92 | 1.021 | 2.88 | 0.916 | 4.262 |
| 55. | 1.25 | 0.515 | 1.40 | 0.952 | 0.750* |
| 56. | 2.44 | 1.498 | 1.96 | 1.231 | 1.600* |
| 57. | 2.48 | 1.548 | 1.29 | 0.656 | 4.507 |
| 58. | 1.51 | 0.917 | 1.44 | 0.831 | 0.286* |
| 59. | 2.44 | 1.422 | 1.37 | 0.554 | 0.265* |
| 60. | 1.92 | 1.086 | 1.70 | 0.974 | 0.833* |

*Difference is insignificant.

The items with 't' ratio less than 1.96 at .05 level of significance were rejected on the ground that they had not discriminatory power.

In this way, item number 5, 6, 19, 27, 28, 29, 33, 38, 45, 55, 56, 58, 59, 60 *i.e.* fourteen items in the total were rejected from the preliminary draft. Item number 46 (Table 4.1) was further retained as its discriminatory power *i.e.* 1.941 is very near to 1.96.

## 4.3 FINAL DRAFT OF THE ROLE CONFLICT SCALE

In the light of the item analysis of the first draft, the final form of the scale was prepared. Out of the sixty items, 14 items were dropped out and 46 items in all were retained.

## 4.4 RELIABILITY

Reliability refers to the consistency of ranks/scores obtained by the same individuals when re-examined with the same test on different tests of equivalent items.

In the present situation, it was difficult to construct a parallel form. Garrett states that "the situation occurs to construct a parallel form with many performance tests, as well as with questionnaires and inventories dealing with personality variables, attitudes and interest."

To test the reliability of this scale split-half method of reliability was used. In this method, even and odd items were splitted and their correlation was computed by applying product moment method. The reliability coefficient of the whole scale was computed with the help of Spearman Brown Prophecy formula :

$$r_{tt} = \frac{2^{r}hh}{1 + r_{hh}}$$

when $r_{tt}$ = reliability of the whole scale

$r_{hh}$ = coefficient of the correlation between the two halves of the scale

The reliability of the whole scale came out to the .85 which was considered satisfactory in case of attitude scale. Guilford (1978) also opines :

"That in practice we expect reliability coefficients to be in the upper brackets of 'r' values usually .70 to .98".

The investigator also computed the area-wise split-half

**Table 4.3. Split-half Reliability Coefficients of Role Conflict Scale for Women Teachers**

| *Sr.No.* | *Role Conflict Areas* | $r_{tt}$ | $\sigma_r$ | *Confidence Limits at Significance Levels* | |
|---|---|---|---|---|---|
| | | | | *at .05 level* | *at .01 level* |
| 1. | Inter Role Conflict | .72 | .09 | .54 to .90 | .49 to .95 |
| 2. | Intra Role Conflict | .66 | .10 | .47 to .85 | .40 to .92 |
| 3. | Family Role Conflict | .64 | .11 | .43 to .85 | .36 to .92 |
| 4. | Job Role Conflcit | .67 | .11 | .46 to .88 | .39 to .95 |
| 5. | Social Role Conflict | .60 | .12 | .37 to .83 | .29 to .91 |
| 6. | Dual Role Conflict | .90 | .03 | .85 to .95 | .82 to .98 |
| 7. | Role Conflict Scale (As a whole) | .85 | .05 | .75 to .94 | .72 to .97 |

reliability coefficients of role conflict. The following reliability coefficients of correlation were found in seven areas and of the scale as a whole (Table 4.3).

## 4.5 VALIDITY

A technique or test is valid if it measures what it claims to measure or what it was intended to measure (Lovell and Lawson, 1907). The validity of the scale was established *i.e.* Face validity, content validity and concurrent validity.

### (*a*) Face Validity

The face validity of the scale was fairly high. There was a close agreement amongst the judges and experts to ensure its face validity.

### (*b*) Content Validity

Content validity examined whether the scale covered all the items adequately from which all the aspects of role conflict were to be assessed. The judges were in consonance with the view that the content was well represented in all the items.

### (*c*) Concurrent Validity

Correlation of a test with a criterian as an external measure is referred to concurrent validity. It was computed by using Teachers' Role Conflict Inventory by Prasad and Bhusan (1991) on 30 women teachers. The obtained validity coefficient of 0.97 was interpreted to be quite satisfactory.

## 4.6 NORMS

Percentile norms were computed. Percentiles are derived scores expressed in terms of percentage of cases below particular scores. A percentile indicates the individual's status in the standardized sample. Lower the percentile, poorer the individual's standing in that particular group.

Percentile norms are shown in Table 4.4.

**Table 4.4. Norms for Role Conflict Scale (RCS)**

| *Sr.No.* | *Scores* | *Percentiles* |
|---|---|---|
| 1. | 150-159 | $P_0$ = 69.50 |

| | | |
|---|---|---|
| 2. | 140-149 | $P_{10}$ = 81.34 |
| 3. | 130-139 | $P_{20}$ = 86.41 |
| 4. | 120-129 | $P_{30}$ = 91.12 |
| 5. | 110-119 | $P_{40}$ = 96.42 |
| 6. | 100-109 | $P_{50}$ = 101.22 |
| 7. | 90-99 | $P_{60}$ = 106.85 |
| 8. | 80-89 | $P_{70}$ = 107.00 |
| 9. | 70-79 | $P_{80}$ = 117.00 |
| | | $P_{90}$ = 124.77 |
| | | $P_{100}$ = 159.50 |

# 5 Distribution of Role Conflict Scores Among Women Teachers

Before the analysis of data, it is necessary to study the nature of the distribution of scores, so that statistical technique can be applied properly. In order to arrive at meaningful conclusions, the analysis of data pertaining to scores of Role Conflict, personality traits and socio-eonomic status with respect to various demographic variables has been made. To study the nature of criterion variable *i.e.* Role Conflict Scores, K-S test is applied as followed :

## 5.1 NATURE OF THE DISTRIBUTION

To study the distribution of role conflict scores in the sample taken, Kolmogorov Smirnov (K-S Test) was used to study the goodness of fit of these scores to a normal distribution. This test was preferred to $X^2$ test of goodness of fit as it is more powerful than the latter. Guilford (1965) has recommended whether this test is applicable, there are good reasons to believe it to be a more sensitive than Chi-square ($X^2$).

This test helps to conclude whether or not a sample score distribution could have arisen by random sampling from a population distributed normally with the same mean and standard deviation as the sample. It gives a standard numerical value which is unaffected by the size of the sample. It also focussses on the largest of deviations. The largest absolute value of $C_{P_o} - C_{P_e}$ is called the maximum deviation D which has been shown in Table 5.1.

$$D = \max (CP_o - CP_e)$$

Where D = maximum deviation

$C_{Po}$ = Observed cumulative proportions

$C_{Pe}$ = Expected cumulative proportions

To find out the significance of statistic for large sample is :

at .05 level of significance $\frac{1.36}{\sqrt{N}}$

at .01 level of significance $\frac{1.63}{\sqrt{N}}$

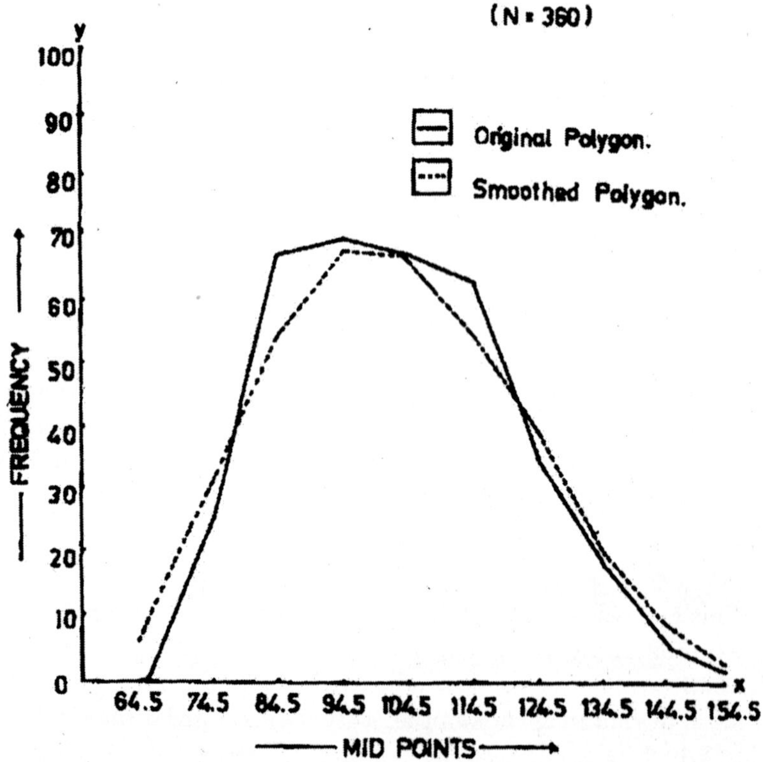


Fig. 5.1. Smoothed Frequency Polygon of Distribution of Role Conflict Scores Among Women Teachers.

D max = 0.0336

N = 360

Table value at .05 level = $\frac{1.36}{\sqrt{N}}$ = .0717

**Table 5.1. Distribution of Role Conflict Scores Among Women Teachers**

By KOLMOGROV – SMIRNOV METHOD (K – S Method)

M = 102.88

O = 17.42

| Sr. No. | Scores | $X_4$ Upper Limit | *f* | *CF* | *x* (X-M) | $Z = \frac{x}{o}$ | $C_{Pe}$ | $C_{Po}$ | $D(C_{Pe} - C_{Po})$ |
|---|---|---|---|---|---|---|---|---|---|
| 1. | 159-159 | 159.5 | 2 | 360 | 56.62 | 3.25 | 1.0000 | 1.0000 | 0.0000 |
| 2. | 140-149 | 149.5 | 6 | 358 | 46.62 | 2.68 | .9963 | .9949 | 0.0019 |
| 3. | 130-139 | 139.5 | 19 | 352 | 36.62 | 2.10 | .9821 | .9778 | 0.0043 |
| 4. | 120-129 | 129.5 | 36 | 333 | 26.62 | 1.53 | .9370 | .9250 | 0.0120 |
| 5. | 110-119 | 119.5 | 64 | 297 | 16.62 | 0.95 | .8290 | .8250 | 0.0040 |
| 6. | 100-109 | 109.5 | 68 | 233 | 6.62 | 0.38 | .6480 | .6472 | 0.0008 |
| 7. | 90-99 | 99.5 | 71 | 165 | −3.38 | 0.19 | .4247 | .4583 | 0.0336 |
| 8. | 80-89 | 89.5 | 68 | 94 | −13.38 | 0.77 | .2406 | .2611 | 0.0205 |
| 9. | 70-79 | 79.5 | 26 | 26 | −23.38 | 1.34 | .0901 | .0722 | 0.0179 |
| 10. | 60-69 | 69.5 | 0 | 0 | −33.38 | 1.92 | .0274 | 0.0000 | 0.0274 |
| 11. | 50-59 | 59.5 | 0 | 0 | −43.38 | 2.49 | .0064 | 0.0000 | 0.0064 |
| 12. | 40-49 | 49.5 | 0 | 0 | −53.38 | 3.06 | .0011 | 0.0000 | 0.0011 |
| | | 360 | | | | | | | |

$$\text{Table value at .01 level} = \frac{1.63}{\sqrt{N}} = 0.0859$$

**Interpretation**

D max. of .0336 is less than the table value *i.e.* 0.0717 at .05 level. So it is not significant at .05 level. It means that the given distribution does not deviate significantly from a normal distribution. Hence, the distribution of role conflict scores in normal among women teachers.

## 5.2 INCIDENCE OF ROLE CONFLICT AMONG WOMEN TEACHERS IN THE TOTAL SAMPLE

The present work proposed to investigate the incidence of role conflict among women teachers in the sample taken. Therefore, to study the incidence of role conflict in the sample, the percentiles ($P_P$) were computed which indicated a particular measurement falling below it. Percentile can be defined as a point in the distribution below which a given percentage of the class lie. Percentile points may be represented by the symbols such as $P_o - P_{100}$. The points $P_o$ and $P_{100}$ are limits which include all the cases of the same distribution. For instance, $P_{50}$ means a point in the distribution which has 50 per cent of the cases lying below it. $P_{50}$ is also known as median or $Q_2$ whereas $P_{25}$ and $P_{75}$ are known as first quartile ($Q_1$) and third quartile ($Q_3$) respectively.

The value of percentiles were computed by the following formula :

$$P_P = 1 + \frac{(P^{N-F})}{f_P} \times i$$

Where P = Percentage of the distribution wanted *e.g.* 10%, 33% etc.

1 = exact lower limit of the class interval upon which $P_P$ lies.

$P^N$ = Part of N to be counted off in order to reach $P_P$

F = Sum of all scores upon intervals below 1

$f_P$ = Number of scores within the interval upon which $P_P$ falls

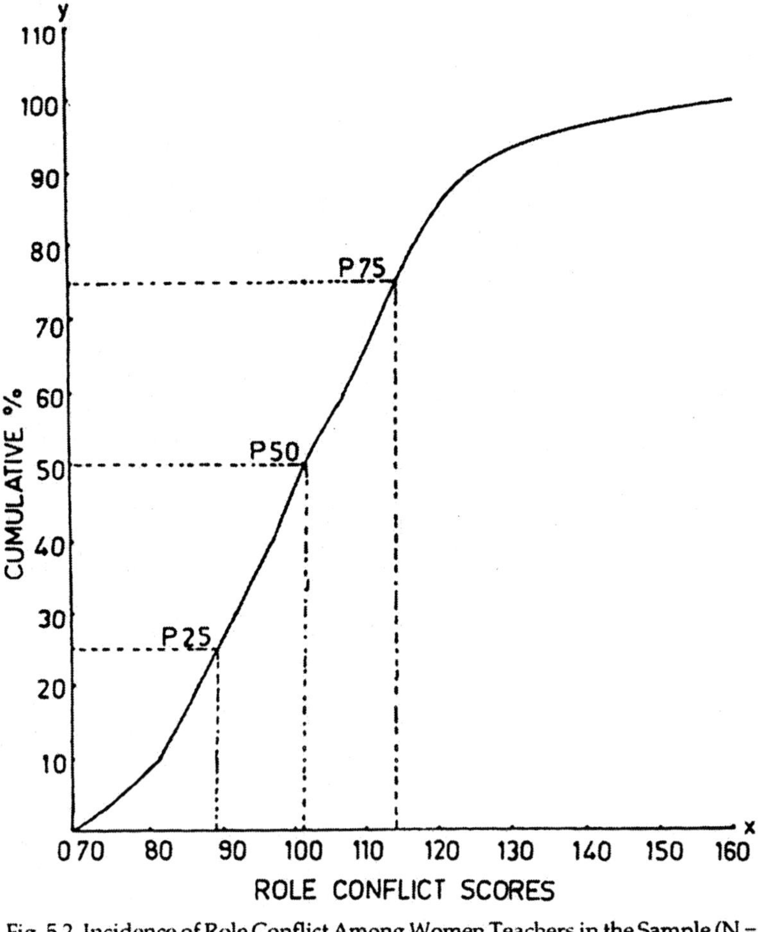


Fig. 5.2. Incidence of Role Conflict Among Women Teachers in the Sample (N = 360).

i = Lenght of the class interval

The computation of various percentiles including mainly $P_{25}$, $P_{50}$ and $P_{75}$ in a frequency distribution of role conflict scores of the sample are shown in Appendix 'J'.

Figure 5.2 shows role conflict among women teachers. It was concluded that 50 per cent of the total class *i.e.* 180 women teachers (50% of 360) scored below 101.22. Above 75 per cent experiencing role conflict scored from 114.40 to 159 and below

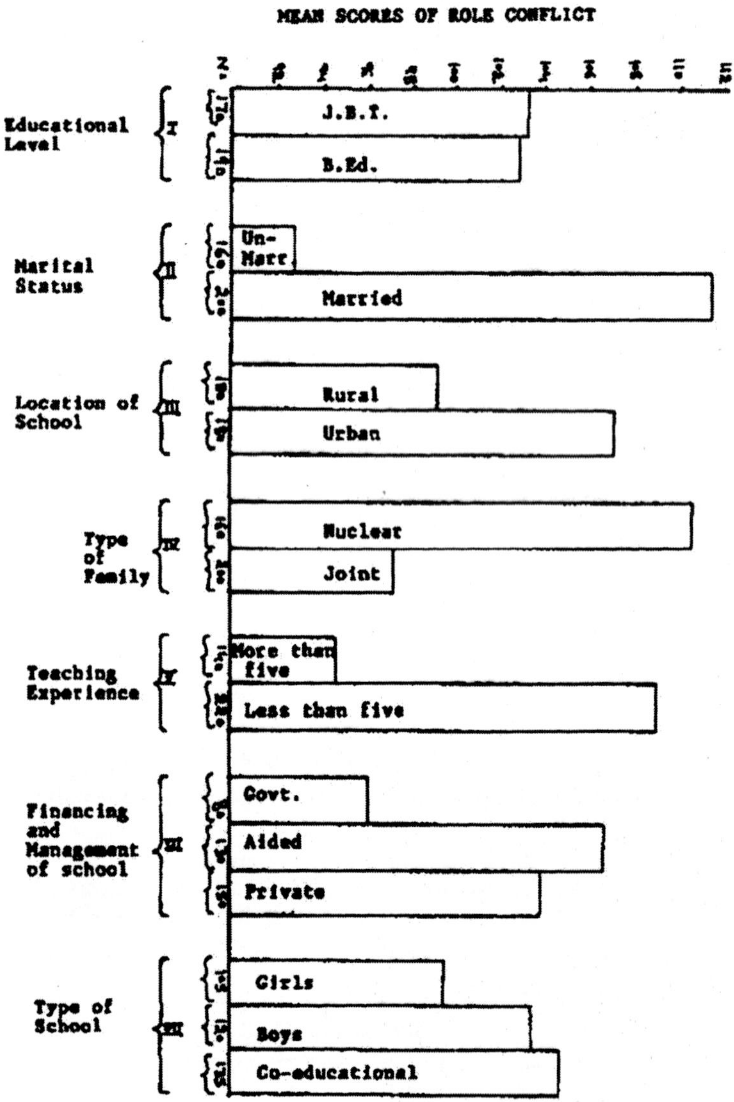


Fig. 5.3. Comparison of Role Conflict Scores Among Women Teachers.

25 per cent experiencing role conflict scored from 69.5 to 88.80. And middle 50 per cent of the cases scored from 88.80 to 114.40. The description of the reslts has been clearly illustrated in Table 5.2.

**Table 5.2. Incidence of Role Conflict Among Women Teachers (N = 360)**

| *Sr. No.* | *Percentage of the cases* | *Role Conflict* | *N* | *Role Conflict score-range* |
|---|---|---|---|---|
| 1. | Above 75% | High | 90 | 114.40 to 159.00 |
| 2. | Middle 50% | Middle | 180 | 88.80 to 114.40 |
| 3. | Below 25% | Low | 90 | 69.50 to 88.80 |

Mean scores of Role Conflict has also been shown in Table 5.3.

**Table 5.3. Mean Scores of Role Conflict Among Women Teachers**

| *Sr. No.* | *Women Teachers* | *Number of Women Teachers* | *Mean Scores of Role Conflict* |
|---|---|---|---|
| *1* | *2* | *3* | *4* |
| 1. | *Educational Qualification* | | |
| | *(a)* J.B.T. | 170 | 103.335 |
| | *(b)* B.Ed. | 190 | 102.905 |
| 2. | *Marital Status* | | |
| | *(a)* Married | 160 | 92.756 |
| | *(b)* Unmarried | 200 | 111.405 |
| 3. | *Location of School* | | |
| | *(a)* Rural | 180 | 99.167 |
| | *(b)* Urban | 180 | 107.050 |
| 4. | *Type of Family* | | |
| | *(a)* Nuclear | 160 | 110.469 |
| | *(b)* Joint | 200 | 97.235 |

*(Contd.)*

*(Contd.)*

| *1* | *2* | *3* | *4* |
|---|---|---|---|
| 5. | *Teaching Experience* | | |
| | *(a)* More than five years | 140 | 94.664 |
| | *(b)* Less than five years | 220 | 108.495 |
| 6. | *Financing and Management of School* | | |
| | *(a)* Government School | 80 | 96.000 |
| | *(b)* Aided School | 130 | 106.592 |
| | *(c)* Private School | 150 | 103.880 |
| 7. | *Type of School* | | |
| | *(a)* Girls School | 105 | 99.438 |
| | *(b)* Boys School | 120 | 103.392 |
| | *(c)* Co-educational school | 135 | 105.711 |

Figure 5.3 shows that married women teachers experience the high role conflict and unmarried women teachers experience the lowest role conflict. The figure reveals that it is the marital status that counts role conflict. No doubt, other variables also effect the level of role conflict.

Educational qualification does not make much difference in the level of role conflict experienced by J.B.T. as well as B.Ed. women teachers. Women teachers working in urban schools experience more role conflict in comparison to the rural women teachers. The figure also reveals very clearly that women teachers belonging to nuclear family experience more role conflict in comparison to women teachers belonging to joint family. Teaching experience also affects a lot the role conflict faced by women teachers. Women teachers having less than five years of teaching experience are prone to high role conflict than those having more than five years of teaching experience.

The figure also shows that women teachers working in aided schools experience more role conflict in comparison to those working in government schools and private schools. It also indicates that women teachers working in co-educational schools also experience more role conflict than those working in girls schools and boys schools.

## 5.3 COMPUTATION OF RELIABILITIES

To judge the workability of 16 Personality Factors Questionnaire and Socio-economic Status Scale on the sample of women teachers included in this study, the investigator selected a sample of 30 respondents from the data randomly with respect to both of these tests. The scores on the tests of these respondents provided the investigator with the required data needed for determining the reliabilities of both the tests.

### *(a)* The Co-efficient of Reliability

Computing the Coefficient of correlation is the usual procedure used to determine the reliability of psychological tests and inventories. There are a number of methods for computing the reliability of the test. Split-half is one of the methods to determine the reliability.

### *(b)* Split-Half Reliabilities

The investigator determined the reliabilities of the Cattell's 16 Personality Factors and Bhardwaj and Gupta's Socio-economic Status Scale among women teachers by Split-half Method on her own sample of 30. In both 16 P.F. and Socio-economic Status Scale, scores of 30 respondents were taken randomly. The items of each of the test were divided dimension-wise into two equal halves using odd-even split. The Pearson's Product Moment Coefficient of correlation was computed by correlating the scores on the odd and even items of the test by using the following formula :

$$r = \frac{N\Sigma XY - (\Sigma X)(\Sigma Y)}{\sqrt{N\Sigma X^2 - (\Sigma X)^2}\sqrt{(N\Sigma Y)^2 - (\Sigma Y)^2}}$$

Where $\Sigma X$ = Sum of X scores

$\Sigma Y$ = Sum of Y scores

$\Sigma X^2$ = Sum of squared X scores

$\Sigma Y^2$ = Sum of squared Y scores

$\Sigma XY$ = Sum of products of X and Y scores

N = Number of paired scores

To estimate the reliability of the full test, Spearman – Brown prophecy formula was used as below.

$$r_{tt} = \frac{2r_{hh}}{1 + r_{hh}}$$

Where $r_{hh}$ = Correlation between halves of a test

$r_{tt}$ = Reliability of a total test

Confidence limits for the coefficient of correlation were computed by the following formula :

$$\sigma_r = \frac{1 - r^2}{\sqrt{N}}$$

Where $\sigma_r$ = Standard error of coefficient of correlation

r = Correlation

N = Number of respondents

Confidence limits = $r \pm \sigma_r \times 1.96$ at .05 level

= $r \pm \sigma_r \times 2.58$ at .01 level

The coefficients of correlation computed for Cattell's 16 Personality Factors and Socio-economic Status Scale among women teachers which are shown in Table Number 5.4 and 5.5 respectively.

**Table 5.4. Split-half Reliability Coefficients for the 16 Personality Factors Among Women Teachers**

| *Personality Factors* | $r_{tt}$ | $\sigma_r$ | *Confidence limits at .05 level* | *Confidence limits at .01 level* |
|---|---|---|---|---|
| *1* | *2* | *3* | *4* | *5* |
| A | .63 | .11 | .41 to .85 | .35 to .93 |
| B | .61 | .11 | .39 to .83 | .33 to .89 |
| C | .68 | .10 | .48 to .88 | .42 to .94 |
| E | .59 | .12 | .35 to .83 | .24 to .90 |
| F | .61 | .11 | .39 to .83 | .33 to .89 |

*(Contd.)*

*(Contd.)*

| *1* | *2* | *3* | *4* | *5* |
|---|---|---|---|---|
| G | .69 | .10 | .51 to .87 | .46 to .92 |
| H | .56 | .13 | .31 to .81 | .22 to .90 |
| I | .58 | .12 | .34 to .82 | .27 to .89 |
| L | .62 | .11 | .40 to .84 | .34 to .90 |
| M | .59 | .12 | .35 to .83 | .28 to .90 |
| N | .64 | .11 | .42 to .86 | .36 to .92 |
| O | .71 | .09 | .53 to .89 | .48 to .94 |
| $Q_1$ | .69 | .09 | .51 to .87 | .46 to .92 |
| $Q_2$ | .67 | .10 | .47 to .87 | .41 to .93 |
| $Q_3$ | .74 | .08 | .58 to .90 | .53 to .95 |
| $Q_4$ | .63 | .11 | .41 to .85 | .35 to .93 |

**Table 5.5. Split-half Reliability Coefficients of Socio-Economic Status Scale for Women Teachers**

| *Sr. No.* | *Areas* | $r_{tt}$ | $\sigma_r$ | *Confidence Limits at .05 level* | *.01 level* |
|---|---|---|---|---|---|
| 1. | Family | .66 | .11 | .41 to .83 | .34 to .90 |
| 2. | Social | .60 | .12 | .37 to .83 | .30 to .90 |
| 3. | Education | .72 | .09 | .54 to .90 | .49 to .95 |
| 4. | Profession | .63 | .11 | .41 to .85 | .35 to .91 |
| 5. | Caste | .88 | .04 | .81 to .95 | .78 to .98 |
| 6. | Total Assests | .64 | .11 | .43 to .85 | .36 to .92 |
| 7. | Monthly Income | .66 | .11 | .41 to .83 | .34 to .90 |
| 8. | Scale (As a whole) | .71 | .09 | .53 to .89 | .48 to .94 |

## Interpretation

The interpretation of correlation is essential in order to estimate about the magnitude of its relationship. The correlation is an index which gives an idea about the association of characteristics between variables. The following factors, however, be kept in view, while interpreting a coefficient of correlation.

The positive value of coefficient of correlation indicates direct relationship and negative value indicates inverse relationship *i.e.* scores in both variables change or vary in opposite directions. The size of the coefficient of correlation indicates the degree of closeness of relationship. The maximum range lies between +1.0 and –1.0. Garrett (1973) has given certain meanings to the value of 'r' (correlation) obtained as such :

*(i)* r from 0.00 to ± 0.20 denotes indifferent or negligible relationship.

*(ii)* r from 0.20 to ± 0.40, low correlation present but slight.

*(iii)* r from ± 0.40 to ± 0.70 denotes substantial or marked relationship.

*(iv)* r from ± 0.70 to 0.80 denotes very high correlation.

Table 5.4 reveals that coefficients range from .56 to .74 for Personality Factors and 5.5 indicates the coefficients range from .60 to .88 for socio-economic Status scores among women teachers.

It is concluded that all the estimated reliabilities of the tests range from substantial to high correlation. The table value of 'r' for significance with 28 df *i.e.* 361 and .463 at .05 and .01 levels respectively. The calculated values of all r's for both tests are greater than .463. Therefore, all the estimated reliabilities are significant at .01 level of significance. It indicates that both the tests are reliable for the sample of women teachers of present study.

# 6 Socio-psychological Correlates of Role Conflict Among Women Teachers

This Chapter deals with the computation of co-efficients of correlation of various Socio-Psychological variables namely—Personality Factors and Socio-economic Status as independent variables whereas role conflict as a dependent variable. It was studied alongwith a number of other variables such as educational level, marital status, location of the school, type of family, teaching experience, financing and management of the school, and type of school among women teachers.

The analysis of the data is carried out in the following sections :

6.1 Coefficients of correlation between Role Conflict, and Personality Factors among women teachers.

6.2 Coefficients of correlation between Role Conflict and Personality Factors with respect to demographic variables.

6.3 Coefficients of correlation between Role Conflict and Socio-economic Status of women teachers.

Coefficients of correlation were computed with the help of Pearson-Product-Moment Method (r).

Significance of correlation coefficients were judged at .05 and .01 levels.

## 6.1 COEFFICIENTS OR CORRELATION BETWEEN ROLE CONFLICT AND PERSONALITY FACTORS AMONG WOMEN TEACHERS

Coefficients of correlation between Role Conflict and personality Factors were calculated in the following sections :

6.1.1 Correlation between Total Role Conflict and Personality Factors.

6.1.2 Correlation between Inter Role Conflict and Personality Factors.

6.1.3 Correlation between Intra Role Conflict and Personality Factors.

6.1.4 Correlation between Family Role Conflict and Personality Factors.

6.1.5 Correlation between Job Role Conflict and Personality Factors.

The obtained results of coefficients of correlation are given in the Table Number 6.1 to 6.5.

**Table 6.1. Coefficients of Correlation Between Total Role Conflict and Personality Factors of Women Teachers**

| *Sr.No.* | *Personality Factors* | *Name of the Factor* | *'r' (Coefficient of Correlation)* |
|---|---|---|---|
| *1* | *2* | *3* | *4* |
| 1. | Reserved Vs. Outgoing | 'A' | –.0503 |
| 2. | Less Intelligent Vs. More Intelligent | 'B' | –.0451 |
| 3. | Emotionally more Stable Vs. Less Stable | 'C' | .0895 |
| 4. | Humble Vs. Assertive | 'E' | –.1839 ** |
| 5. | Sober Vs. Happy-go-lucky | 'F' | .0113 |
| 6. | Expedient Vs. Conscientious | 'G' | .2817 ** |
| 7. | Shy Vs. Venturesome | 'H' | .1433 ** |
| 8. | Tough Vs. Tender-minded | 'I' | –.0595 |
| 9. | Trusting Vs. Suspicious | 'L' | .2539 ** |
| 10. | Practical Vs. Imaginative | 'M' | .0695 |
| 11. | Forthright Vs. Shrewd | 'N' | –.0286 |
| 12. | Untroubled Vs. Troubled | 'O' | .1043 |
| 13. | Conservative Vs. Liberal | '$Q_1$' | –.006 |

*(Contd.)*

*(Contd.)*

| 1 | 2 | 3 | 4 |
|---|---|---|---|
| 14. | Group Dependent Vs. Self Sufficient | '$Q_2$' | .2038 ** |
| 15. | Undisciplined Vs. Controlled | '$Q_3$' | .1910 ** |
| 16. | Relaxed Vs. Tense | '$Q_4$' | –.1731 ** |

*Significant at .01 level. N = 360

df = 358

Table value at .05 level of significance = .105

Table value at .01 level of significance = .138

Table 6.1 reveals that the coefficients of correlation between Role Conflict and Personality Factors E, G, H, L, $Q_2$, $Q_3$, and $Q_4$ are significant.

There are positive correlations between Role conflict and personality factors G, H, L, $Q_2$ and $Q_3$ which are significant at .01 level. It shows that Personality Factor conscientious, venturesome, suspicious, self sufficient and controlled lead to increase the Role Conflict.

There are negative correlations between Role Conflict and Personality Factors E and $Q_4$ which are significant at .01 level. It shows that humble and relaxed persons experience high Role Conflict.

Rest of the correlations between Role Conflict and Personality Factors A, B, C, F, I, M, N, O and $Q_1$ are insignificant. It shows that there exists no relationship between Role Conflict and the Personality Factors.

**Table 6.2. Coefficients of Correlation Between Inter Role Conflict and Personality Factors of Women Teachers**

| *Sr.No.* | *Personality Factors* | *Name of the Factor* | *'r' (Coefficient of Correlation)* |
|---|---|---|---|
| *1* | *2* | *3* | *4* |
| 1. | Reserved Vs. Outgoing | 'A' | –.0301 |

*(Contd.)*

*(Contd.)*

| *1* | *2* | *3* | *4* |
|---|---|---|---|
| 2. | Less Intelligent Vs. More Intelligent | 'B' | –.0365 |
| 3. | Emotionally more Stable Vs. Less Stable | 'C' | .1494 ** |
| 4. | Humble Vs. Assertive | 'E' | –.0521 |
| 5. | Sober Vs. Happy-go-lucky | 'F' | .0390 |
| 6. | Expedient Vs. Conscientious | 'G' | .1777 ** |
| 7. | Shy Vs. Venturesome | 'H' | .1536 ** |
| 8. | Tough Vs. Tender-minded | 'I' | –.0593 |
| 9. | Trusting Vs. Suspicious | 'L' | .1592 ** |
| 10. | Practical Vs. Imaginative | 'M' | .0792 |
| 11. | Forthright Vs. Shrewd | 'N' | –.0901 |
| 12. | Untroubled Vs. Troubled | 'O' | –.0092 |
| 13. | Conservative Vs. Liberal | '$Q_1$' | .0402 |
| 14. | Group Dependent Vs. Self Sufficient | '$Q_2$' | .1662 ** |
| 15. | Undisciplined Vs. Controlled | '$Q_3$' | .2701 ** |
| 16. | Relaxed Vs. Tense | '$Q_4$' | –.1447 ** |

**Significant at .01 level. N = 360

df = 358

Table value at .05 level of significance = .105

Table value at .01 level of significance = .138

Table 6.2 reveals that the coefficients of correlation between inter Role Conflict and Personality Factors C, G, H, L, $Q_2$, $Q_3$, and $Q_4$ are significant.

There are positive correlations between inter Role Conflict and Personality factors C, G, H, L, $Q_2$ and $Q_3$ which are significant at .01 level. It shows that Personality Factor emotionally, less stable, conscientious, venturesome, suspicious, self sufficient and controlled lead to increase the inter Role Conflict.

There is negative correlation between inter Role Conflict and Personality Factor $Q_4$ which is significant at .01 level. It shows that relaxed women teachers experience higher inter Role Conflict.

Rest of the correlation between inter Role Conflict and Personality Factors A, B, E, F, I, M, N, O and $Q_1$ are insignificant.

**Table 6.3. Coefficients of Correlation Between Intra Role Conflict and Personality Factors of Women Teachers**

| *Sr.No.* | *Personality Factors* | *Name of the Factor* | *'r' (Coefficient of Correlation)* |
|---|---|---|---|
| *1* | *2* | *3* | *4* |
| 1. | Reserved Vs. Outgoing | 'A' | –.1398 ** |
| 2. | Less Intelligent Vs. More Intelligent | 'B' | .0054 |
| 3. | Emotionally more Stable Vs. Less Stable | 'C' | –.0531 |
| 4. | Humble Vs. Assertive | 'E' | –.2756 ** |
| 5. | Sober Vs. Happy-go-lucky | 'F' | –.0363 |
| 6. | Expedient Vs. Conscientious | 'G' | .2732 ** |
| 7. | Shy Vs. Venturesome | 'H' | .0416 |
| 8. | Tough Vs. Tender-minded | 'I' | –.0113 |
| 9. | Trusting Vs. Suspicious | 'L' | .2337 ** |
| 10. | Practical Vs. Imaginative | 'M' | –.0059 |
| 11. | Forthright Vs. Shrewd | 'N' | .0913 |
| 12. | Untroubled Vs. Troubled | 'O' | .2052 ** |
| 13. | Conservative Vs. Liberal | '$Q_1$' | –.0704 |
| 14. | Group Dependent Vs. Self Sufficient | '$Q_2$' | .1380 ** |
| 15. | Undisciplined Vs. Controlled | '$Q_3$' | –.0529 |
| 16. | Relaxed Vs. Tense | '$Q_4$' | –.1107 * |

*Significant at .05 level.
**Significant at .01 level. N = 360
df = 358

Table value at .05 level of significance = .105
Table value at .01 level of significance = .138

Table 6.3 reveals that the coefficients of correlation between Intra Role Conflict and Personality Factors A, E, G, L, O, $Q_2$, and $Q_4$ are significant.

There are positive correlations between Intra Role Conflict and Personality Factors G, L, O, and $Q_1$ which are significant at .01 level. It shows that Personality Factors, conscientious, suspicious troubled and self-sufficient lead to increase the Intra Role Conflict.

There are negative correlations between Intra Role Conflict and Personality Factors A, E, and $Q_4$ which are significant at .01 level. It shows that reserved, humble and relaxed women experience high Intra Role Conflict.

Rest of the correlations between Personality Factors B, C, F, H, I, M, N, $Q_1$, $Q_3$ and Intra Role Conflict are insignificant.

**Table 6.4. Coefficients of Correlation Between Family Role Conflict and Personality Factors of Women Teachers**

| *Sr.No.* | *Personality Factors* | *Name of the Factor* | *'r' (Coefficient of Correlation)* |
|---|---|---|---|
| *1* | *2* | *3* | *4* |
| 1. | Reserved Vs. Outgoing | 'A' | –.0065 |
| 2. | Less Intelligent Vs. More Intelligent | 'B' | –.0040 |
| 3. | Emotionally more Stable Vs. Less Stable | 'C' | .1078 * |
| 4. | Humble Vs. Assertive | 'E' | –.1222 * |
| 5. | Sober Vs. Happy-go-lucky | 'F' | –.0064 |
| 6. | Expedient Vs. Conscientious | 'G' | .2265 ** |
| 7. | Shy Vs. Venturesome | 'H' | .1106 |
| 8. | Tough Vs. Tender-minded | 'I' | –.0725 |
| 9. | Trusting Vs. Suspicious | 'L' | .1787 ** |
| 10. | Practical Vs. Imaginative | 'M' | .1064 * |
| 11. | Forthright Vs. Shrewd | 'N' | –.0319 |
| 12. | Untroubled Vs. Troubled | 'O' | –.0974 |

*(Contd.)*

*(Contd.)*

| *1* | *2* | *3* | *4* |
|---|---|---|---|
| 13. | Conservative Vs. Liberal | '$Q_1$' | .0230 |
| 14. | Group Dependent Vs. Self Sufficient | '$Q_2$' | .1442 ** |
| 15. | Undisciplined Vs. Controlled | '$Q_3$' | .1863 ** |
| 16. | Relaxed Vs. Tense | '$Q_4$' | –.1494 ** |

*Significant at .05 level. N = 360

**Significant at .01 level. df = 358

Table value at .05 level of significance = .105.

Table value at .01 level of significance = .138.

Table 6.4 reveals that the coefficients of correlation between family Role Conflict and Personality Factors C, E, G, H, L, M, $Q_2$, $Q_3$, and $Q_4$ are significant.

There are positive correlations between family Role Conflict and Personality factors C, H, and M which are significant at .05 level. It also reveals that there exists positive correlations between family Role Conflict and Personality Factors G, L, $Q_2$ and $Q_3$ which are significant at .01 level. It shows that emotionally less stable, venturesome, imaginative, conscientious, suspicious, self-sufficient and controlled lead to high family Role Conflict.

There are negative correlations between family Role Conflict and Personality Factors E and $Q_4$ which are significant at .05 level and .01 level respectively. It shows that humble and relaxed women teachers experience high family shows that humble and relaxed women teachers experience high family Role Conflict.

Rest of the correlations between family Role Conflict and Personality Factors A, B, F, I, N, O and $Q_1$ and insignificant.

**Table 6.5. Coefficients of Correlation Between Job Role Conflict and Personality Factors of Women Teachers**

| *Sr.No.* | *Personality Factors* | *Name of the Factor* | *'r' (Coefficient of Correlation)* |
|---|---|---|---|
| *1* | *2* | *3* | *4* |
| 1. | Reserved Vs. Outgoing | 'A' | –.0620 |
| 2. | Less Intelligent Vs. More Intelligent | 'B' | –.0080 |
| 3. | Emotionally more Stable Vs. Less Stable | 'C' | .0624 |
| 4. | Humble Vs. Assertive | 'E' | –.2049 ** |
| 5. | Sober Vs. Happy-go-lucky | 'F' | .0383 |
| 6. | Expedient Vs. Conscientious | 'G' | .2603 ** |
| 7. | Shy Vs. Venturesome | 'H' | .1513 ** |
| 8. | Tough Vs. Tender-minded | 'I' | –.0089 |
| 9. | Trusting Vs. Suspicious | 'L' | .2177 ** |
| 10. | Practical Vs. Imaginative | 'M' | –0149 |
| 11. | Forthright Vs. Shrewd | 'N' | –.0812 |
| 12. | Untroubled Vs. Troubled | 'O' | .0839 |
| 13. | Conservative Vs. Liberal | '$Q_1$' | –.0575 |
| 14. | Group Dependent Vs. Self Sufficient | '$Q_2$' | .1793 ** |
| 15. | Undisciplined Vs. Controlled | '$Q_3$' | .1173 * |
| 16. | Relaxed Vs. Tense | '$Q_4$' | –.1339 * |

*Significant at .05 level. N = 360

**Significant at .01 level. df = 358

Table value at .05 level of significance = .105.

Table value at .01 level of significance = .138.

Table 6.5 reveals that the coefficients of correlation between job Role Conflict and Personality Factors E, G, H, L, $Q_2$, $Q_3$ and $Q_4$ are significant.

There are positive correlations between job Role Conflict and Personality Factors G, H, L and $Q_2$ which are significant at .01 level. There is also a positive correlation between job Role Conflict and Personality Factor $Q_3$ which is significant at .05 level. It shows that Personality Factors conscientious, venturesome, suspicious, self sufficient and controlled lead to high job Role Conflict.

There are negative correlations between job Role Conflict and Personality Factors E and $Q_4$ which are significant at .01 level and .05 level respectively. It shows that humble and relaxed women teachers experience high job Role Conflict.

Rest of the correlations between job Role Conflict and Personality Factors A, B, C, F, I, M, N, O and $Q_1$ are insignificant.

## 6.2 COEFFICIENTS OF CORRELATION BETWEEN ROLE CONFLICT AND PERSONALITY FACTORS WITH RESPECT TO DEMOGRAPHIC VARIABLES

Coefficients of correlation between Role Conflict and Personality Factors with respect to educational level, marital status, location of the school, type of family, teaching experience, financing and management of school, and type of school were calculated in the following sections :

6.2.1 Correlation between Role Conflict and Personality Factors with respect to **educational level**.

*(a)* Correlation between Role Conflict and Personality Factors of J.B.T. Women Teachers.

*(b)* Correlation between Role Conflict and Personality Factors of B.Ed. Women teachers.

6.2.2 Correlation between Role Conflict and Personality Factors with respect to **marital status**.

*(a)* Correlation Between Role Conflict and Personality Factors of married women teachers.

*(b)* Correlation between Role Conflict and Personality Factors of unmarried women teachers.

6.2.3 Correlation between Role Conflict and Personality Factors with respect to **location of the school**.

*(a)* Correlation between Role Conflict and Personality Factors of women teachers teaching in rural areas.

*(b)* Correlation between Role Conflict and Personality Factors of women teachers teaching in urban areas.

6.2.4 Correlation between Role Conflict and Personality Factors with respect to **type of family**.

*(a)* Correlation between Role Conflict and Personality Factors of women teachers belonging to nuclear family.

*(b)* Correlation between Role Conflict and Personality Factors of women teachers belonging to joint family.

6.2.5 Correlation between Role Conflict and Personality Factors with respect to **teaching experience**.

*(a)* Correlation between Role Conflict and Personality Factors of women teachers having more than five years of teaching experience.

*(b)* Correlation between Role Conflict and Personality Factors of women teachers having less than five years of teaching experience.

6.2.6 Correlation between Role Conflict and Personality Factors with respect to **financing and management of school**.

*(a)* Correlation between Role Conflict and Personality Factors of women teachers teaching in government schools.

*(b)* Correlation between Role Conflict and Personality Factors of women teachers teaching in aided schools.

*(c)* Correlation between Role Conflict and

Personality Factors of women teachers teaching in private schools.

6.2.7 Correlation between Role Conflict and Personality Factors with respect to **type of school**.

(a) Correlation between Role Conflict and Personality Factors of women teachers teaching in girls schools.

(b) Correlation between Role Conflict and Personality Factors of women teachers teaching in boys schools.

(c) Correlation between Role Conflict and Personality Factors of women teachers teaching in co-educational schools.

The obtained results of coefficients of correlation are given in the Table Number 6.6 to 6.21.

**Table 6.6. Coefficients of Correlation Between Role Conflict and Personality Factors of J.B.T. Women Teachers**

| *Sr.No.* | *Personality Factors* | *Name of the Factor* | *'r' (Coefficient of Correlation)* |
|---|---|---|---|
| *1* | *2* | *3* | *4* |
| 1. | Reserved Vs. Outgoing | 'A' | –.1179 |
| 2. | Less Intelligent Vs. More Intelligent | 'B' | .0734 |
| 3. | Emotionally more Stable Vs. Less Stable | 'C' | .2328 |
| 4. | Humble Vs. Assertive | 'E' | –.1493 * |
| 5. | Sober Vs. Happy-go-lucky | 'F' | .0258 |
| 6. | Expedient Vs. Conscientious | 'G' | .1814 * |
| 7. | Shy Vs. Venturesome | 'H' | –.1002 |
| 8. | Tough Vs. Tender-minded | 'I' | –.0340 |
| 9. | Trusting Vs. Suspicious | 'L' | .1200 |
| 10. | Practical Vs. Imaginative | 'M' | .0295 |
| 11. | Forthright Vs. Shrewd | 'N' | –.1363 |

*(Contd.)*

*(Contd.)*

| *1* | *2* | *3* | *4* |
|---|---|---|---|
| 12. | Untroubled Vs. Troubled | 'O' | .1354 |
| 13. | Conservative Vs. Liberal | '$Q_1$' | –.0702 |
| 14. | Group Dependent Vs. Self Sufficient | '$Q_2$' | .1332 |
| 15. | Undisciplined Vs. Controlled | '$Q_3$' | .1988 ** |
| 16. | Relaxed Vs. Tense | '$Q_4$' | –.1764 * |

*Significant at .05 level. N = 360

**Significant at .01 level. df = 358

Table value at .05 level of significance = .1485.

Table value at .01 level of significance = .1945.

Table 6.6 reveals that coefficients of correlation between Role Conflict and Personality Factors E, G, $Q_3$ and $Q_4$ of J.B.T. women teachers are significant.

There are positive correlations between Role Conflict and Personality Factors G and $Q_3$ which are significant at .05 level and .01 level respectively. It shows that Personality Factors conscientious and controlled lead to increase the Role Conflict.

There are negative correlations between Role Conflict and Personality Factors E and $Q_4$ which are significant at .05 level. It shows that humble and relaxed women teachers experience high Role Conflict.

Rest of the correlations between Role Conflict and Personality Factors A, B, C, F, H, I, L, M, N, O, $Q_1$ and $Q_2$ are insignificant.

**Table 6.7. Coefficients of Correlation Between Role Conflict and Personality Factors of B.Ed. Women Teachers**

| *Sr.No.* | *Personality Factors* | *Name of the Factor* | *'r' (Coefficient of Correlation)* |
|---|---|---|---|
| *1* | *2* | *3* | *4* |
| 1. | Reserved Vs. Outgoing | 'A' | –.0474 |

*(Contd.)*

*(Contd.)*

| *1* | *2* | *3* | *4* |
|---|---|---|---|
| 2. | Less Intelligent Vs. More Intelligent | 'B' | –.2532 ** |
| 3. | Emotionally more Stable Vs. Less Stable | 'C' | .0650 |
| 4. | Humble Vs. Assertive | 'E' | –.0970 |
| 5. | Sober Vs. Happy-go-lucky | 'F' | .0849 |
| 6. | Expedient Vs. Conscientious | 'G' | .2302 ** |
| 7. | Shy Vs. Venturesome | 'H' | .2826 ** |
| 8. | Tough Vs. Tender-minded | 'I' | .0560 |
| 9. | Trusting Vs. Suspicious | 'L' | .2542 ** |
| 10. | Practical Vs. Imaginative | 'M' | .1316 |
| 11. | Forthright Vs. Shrewd | 'N' | –.0595 |
| 12. | Untroubled Vs. Troubled | 'Q' | .0040 |
| 13. | Conservative Vs. Liberal | '$Q_1$' | .1653 * |
| 14. | Group Dependent Vs. Self Sufficient | '$Q_2$' | .1995 ** |
| 15. | Undisciplined Vs. Controlled | '$Q_3$' | .2004 ** |
| 16. | Relaxed Vs. Tense | '$Q_4$' | .1117 |

*Significant at .05 level.

**Significant at .01 level.

Table value at .05 level of significance = .1485.

Table value at .01 level of significance = .1945.

Table 6.7 reveals that coefficients of correlation between Role Conflict and Personality Factors B, G, H, L, $Q_1$, $Q_2$ and $Q_3$ of B.Ed women teachers are significant.

There are positive correlations between Role Conflict and Personality Factors G, H, L, $Q_2$ and $Q_3$ which are significant at .01 level. There is also a positive correlation between Role Conflict and Personality Factor $Q_1$ which is significant at .05 level. It shows that conscientious, venturesome, suspicious, self sufficient, controlled and liberal lead to high Role Conflict.

There is a negative correlation between Role Conflict and Personality Factor B which is significant at .01 level. It shows that dull B.Ed. women teachers experience high Role Conflict.

Rest of the correlations between Role Conflict and Personality Factors A, C, E, F, I, M, N, O and $Q_4$ are insignificant.

**Table 6.8. Coefficients of Correlation Between Role Conflict and Personality Factors of Married Women Teachers**

| *Sr.No.* | *Personality Factors* | *Name of the Factor* | *'r' (Coefficient of Correlation)* |
|---|---|---|---|
| *1* | *2* | *3* | *4* |
| 1. | Reserved Vs. Outgoing | 'A' | –.0569 |
| 2. | Less Intelligent Vs. More Intelligent | 'B' | –.0211 |
| 3. | Emotionally more Stable Vs. Less Stable | 'C' | .0041 |
| 4. | Humble Vs. Assertive | 'E' | .0260 |
| 5. | Sober Vs. Happy-go-lucky | 'F' | .0107 |
| 6. | Expedient Vs. Conscientious | 'G' | .1372 |
| 7. | Shy Vs. Venturesome | 'H' | .0575 |
| 8. | Tough Vs. Tender-minded | 'I' | –.1719 * |
| 9. | Trusting Vs. Suspicious | 'L' | .0861 |
| 10. | Practical Vs. Imaginative | 'M' | .1204 |
| 11. | Forthright Vs. Shrewd | 'N' | .0618 |
| 12. | Untroubled Vs. Troubled | 'O' | .0008 |
| 13. | Conservative Vs. Liberal | '$Q_1$' | –.0046 |
| 14. | Group Dependent Vs. Self Sufficient | '$Q_2$' | –.0672 |
| 15. | Undisciplined Vs. Controlled | '$Q_3$' | –.1309 |
| 16. | Relaxed Vs. Tense | '$Q_4$' | .0732 |

*Significant at .05 level. N = 200

df = 198

Table value at .05 level of significance = .1485.

Table value at .01 level of significance = .1945.

*means less intelligent.

Table 6.8 reveals that the coefficient of correlation between Role Conflict and Personality Factor 'I' is significant at .05 level. It also reveals that there is a negative correlation between Role Conflict and Personality Factor 'I' of married women teachers. It shows that tough minded married women teachers experience high Role Conflict.

Rest of the correlations between Role Conflict and Personality Factors A, B, C, E, F, G, H, L, M, N, O, $Q_1$, $Q_2$, $Q_3$ and $Q_4$ are insignificant.

**Table 6.9. Coefficients of Correlation Between Role Conflict and Personality Factors of Unmarried Women Teachers**

| *Sr.No.* | *Personality Factors* | *Name of the Factor* | *'r' (Coefficient of Correlation)* |
|---|---|---|---|
| *1* | *2* | *3* | *4* |
| 1. | Reserved Vs. Outgoing | 'A' | –.1861 * |
| 2. | Less Intelligent Vs. More Intelligent | 'B' | –.1273 |
| 3. | Emotionally more Stable Vs. Less Stable | 'C' | –.0347 |
| 4. | Humble Vs. Assertive | 'E' | .0165 |
| 5. | Sober Vs. Happy-go-lucky | 'F' | –.0258 |
| 6. | Expedient Vs. Conscientious | 'G' | –.0597 |
| 7. | Shy Vs. Venturesome | 'H' | –.0239 |
| 8. | Tough Vs. Tender-minded | 'I' | –.1370 |
| 9. | Trusting Vs. Suspicious | 'L' | .0935 |
| 10. | Practical Vs. Imaginative | 'M' | .0340 |
| 11. | Forthright Vs. Shrewd | 'N' | .1201 |
| 12. | Untroubled Vs. Troubled | 'O' | –.0252 |
| 13. | Conservative Vs. Liberal | '$Q_1$' | .0492 |
| 14. | Group Dependent Vs. Self Sufficient | '$Q_2$' | .0621 |
| 15. | Undisciplined Vs. Controlled | '$Q_3$' | .1334 |
| 16. | Relaxed Vs. Tense | '$Q_4$' | .0131 |

*Significant at .05 level. N = 200

df = 158

Table value at .05 level of significance = .1485.

Table value at .01 level of significance = .1945.

Table 6.9 reveals that there is a negative correlation between Role Conflict and Personality Factor 'A' which is significant at .05 level. It means that reserved unmarried women teachers experiences high Role Conflict.

Rest of the correlations between Role Conflict and Personality Factors B, C, E, F, G, H, I, L, M, N, O, $Q_1$, $Q_2$, $Q_3$ and $Q_4$ are insignificant.

**Table 6.10. Coefficients of Correlation Between Role Conflict and Personality Factors of Women Teachers Teaching in Rural Areas**

| *Sr.No.* | *Personality Factors* | *Name of the Factor* | *'r' (Coefficient of Correlation)* |
|---|---|---|---|
| *1* | *2* | *3* | *4* |
| 1. | Reserved Vs. Outgoing | 'A' | –.0968 |
| 2. | Less Intelligent Vs. More Intelligent | 'B' | .1186 |
| 3. | Emotionally more Stable Vs. Less Stable | 'C' | –.1416 |
| 4. | Humble Vs. Assertive | 'E' | –.0099 |
| 5. | Sober Vs. Happy-go-lucky | 'F' | –.1526 * |
| 6. | Expedient Vs. Conscientious | 'G' | .2009 ** |
| 7. | Shy Vs. Venturesome | 'H' | .0928 |
| 8. | Tough Vs. Tender-minded | 'I' | .0334 |
| 9. | Trusting Vs. Suspicious | 'L' | .1057 |
| 10. | Practical Vs. Imaginative | 'M' | .1639 * |
| 11. | Forthright Vs. Shrewd | 'N' | .2011 ** |
| 12. | Untroubled Vs. Troubled | 'O' | .1718 * |
| 13. | Conservative Vs. Liberal | '$Q_1$' | .0088 |
| 14. | Group Dependent Vs. Self Sufficient | '$Q_2$' | .0533 |
| 15. | Undisciplined Vs. Controlled | '$Q_3$' | –.0161 |
| 16. | Relaxed Vs. Tense | '$Q_4$' | –.1714 * |

*Significant at .05 level. N = 180

**Significant at .01 level. df = 178

Table value at .05 level of significance = .1485.

Table value at .01 level of significance = .1945.

Table 6.10 reveals that coefficients of correlation between Role Conflict and Personality Factor F, G, M, N, O and $Q_4$ are significant.

There are positive correlations between Role Conflict and Personality Factor G and N which are significant at 0.1 level. There are also positive correlations between Role Conflict and Personality Factors M and O which are significant at .05 level. All this shows that Personality Factors conscientious, shrewdness, imaginative and apprehensive lead to increase high Role Conflict.

There are negative correlations between Role Conflict and Personality Factors F and $Q_4$ which are significant at .05 level. It shows that sober and relaxed women teachers teaching in rural areas experience high Role Conflict.

Rest of the correlations between Role Conflict and Personality Factors A, B,C, E, H, I, L, $Q_1$, $Q_2$, and $Q_3$ are insignificant.

**Table 6.11. Coefficients of Correlation Between Role Conflict and Personality Factors of Women Teachers Teaching if Urban Areas**

| *Sr.No.* | *Personality Factors* | *Name of the Factor* | *'r' (Coefficient of Correlation)* |
|---|---|---|---|
| *1* | *2* | *3* | *4* |
| 1. | Reserved Vs. Outgoing | 'A' | –.0697 |
| 2. | Less Intelligent Vs. More Intelligent | 'B' | –.1821 * |
| 3. | Emotionally more Stable Vs. Less Stable | 'C' | –.0047 |
| 4. | Humble Vs. Assertive | 'E' | –.0295 |
| 5. | Sober Vs. Happy-go-lucky | 'F' | .1405 |
| 6. | Expedient Vs. Conscientious | 'G' | .0094 |
| 7. | Shy Vs. Venturesome | 'H' | .0274 |
| 8. | Tough Vs. Tender-minded | 'I' | .0142 |
| 9. | Trusting Vs. Suspicious | 'L' | .1868 * |
| 10. | Practical Vs. Imaginative | 'M' | .1722 * |

*(Contd.)*

*(Contd.)*

| *1* | *2* | *3* | *4* |
|---|---|---|---|
| 11. | Forthright Vs. Shrewd | 'N' | –.0034 |
| 12. | Untroubled Vs. Troubled | 'O' | .0318 |
| 13. | Conservative Vs. Liberal | '$Q_1$' | .1498 * |
| 14. | Group Dependent Vs. Self Sufficient | '$Q_2$' | –.0479 |
| 15. | Undisciplined Vs. Controlled | '$Q_3$' | .0460 |
| 16. | Relaxed Vs. Tense | '$Q_4$' | .0629 |

*Significant at .05 level. N = 180
df = 178
Table value at .05 level of significance = .1485.
Table value at .01 level of significance = .1945.

Table 6.11 reveals that the coefficients of correlation between Role Conflict and Personality Factors B, L, M and $Q_1$ are significant.

There are positive correlation between Role Conflict and Personality Factors L, M, and $Q_1$ which are significant at .05 level. It shows that Personality Factors suspicious, imaginative and liberal lead to increase the Role Conflict.

There is a negative correlation between Role Conflict and Personality Factor 'B', which is significant at .05 level. It shows that dull women teachers teaching in urban schools experience high Role Conflict.

Rest of the correlations between Role Conflict and Personality Factors A, C, E, F, G, H, I, N, O, $Q_2$, $Q_3$ and $Q_4$ are insignificant.

**Table 6.12. Coefficients of Correlation Between Role Conflict and Personality Factors of Women Teachers Belonging to Nuclear Family**

| *Sr.No.* | *Personality Factors* | *Name of the Factor* | *'r' (Coefficient of Correlation)* |
|---|---|---|---|
| *1* | *2* | *3* | *4* |
| 1. | Reserved Vs. Outgoing | 'A' | –.0572 |

*(Contd.)*

*means less intelligent.

*(Contd.)*

| *1* | *2* | *3* | *4* |
|---|---|---|---|
| 2. | Less Intelligent Vs. More Intelligent | 'B' | –.2051 ** |
| 3. | Emotionally more Stable Vs. Less Stable | 'C' | –.0690 |
| 4. | Humble Vs. Assertive | 'E' | –.0147 |
| 5. | Sober Vs. Happy-go-lucky | 'F' | .1424 |
| 6. | Expedient Vs. Conscientious | 'G' | .0303 |
| 7. | Shy Vs. Venturesome | 'H' | .0447 |
| 8. | Tough Vs. Tender-minded | 'I' | –.0082 |
| 9. | Trusting Vs. Suspicious | 'L' | .1260 |
| 10. | Practical Vs. Imaginative | 'M' | .1030 |
| 11. | Forthright Vs. Shrewd | 'N' | –.0202 |
| 12. | Untroubled Vs. Troubled | 'O' | .0694 |
| 13. | Conservative Vs. Liberal | '$Q_1$' | .1258 |
| 14. | Group Dependent Vs. Self Sufficient | '$Q_2$' | –.0539 |
| 15. | Undisciplined Vs. Controlled | '$Q_3$' | .0098 |
| 16. | Relaxed Vs. Tense | '$Q_4$' | .0836 |

**Significant at .05 level. N = 160

df = 158

Table value at .05 level of significance = .1485.

Table value at .01 level of significance = .1945.

Table 6.12 reveals that the Coefficient of correlation between Role Conflict and Personality Factor 'B' is negative which is significant at .01 level. It shows that dull* women teachers belonging to nuclear family experience high Role Conflict.

Rest of the correlations between Role Conflict and Personality Factor A, C, E, F, G, H, I, L, M, N, O, $Q_1$, $Q_2$, $Q_3$ and $Q_4$ are insignificant.

*means less intelligent.

**Table 6.13. Coefficients of Correlation Between Role Conflict and Personality Factors of Women Teachers Belonging to Joint Family**

| *Sr.No.* | *Personality Factors* | *Name of the Factor* | *'r' (Coefficient of Correlation)* |
|---|---|---|---|
| *1* | *2* | *3* | *4* |
| 1. | Reserved Vs. Outgoing | 'A' | –.0256 |
| 2. | Less Intelligent Vs. More Intelligent | 'B' | –.1636 * |
| 3. | Emotionally more Stable Vs. Less Stable | 'C' | –.0644 |
| 4. | Humble Vs. Assertive | 'E' | –.0487 |
| 5. | Sober Vs. Happy-go-lucky | 'F' | –.1569 * |
| 6. | Expedient Vs. Conscientious | 'G' | .1867 * |
| 7. | Shy Vs. Venturesome | 'H' | .0341 |
| 8. | Tough Vs. Tender-minded | 'I' | .0237 |
| 9. | Trusting Vs. Suspicious | 'L' | .1195 |
| 10. | Practical Vs. Imaginative | 'M' | .1577 * |
| 11. | Forthright Vs. Shrewd | 'N' | .2282 ** |
| 12. | Untroubled Vs. Troubled | 'O' | .1445 |
| 13. | Conservative Vs. Liberal | '$Q_1$' | –.0273 |
| 14. | Group Dependent Vs. Self Sufficient | '$Q_2$' | .0753 |
| 15. | Undisciplined Vs. Controlled | '$Q_3$' | .0117 |
| 16. | Relaxed Vs. Tense | '$Q_4$' | –.1896 * |

*Significant at .05 level. N = 200

**Significant at .01 level. df = 198

Table value at .05 level of significance = .1485.

Table value at .01 level of significance = .1945.

Table 6.13 reveals that the coefficients of correlation between Role Conflict and Personality Factor B, F, G, M, N and $Q_4$ are significant.

There are positive correlations between Role Conflict and Personality Factors B, G, and M which are significant at .05

level. There is also a positive correlation between Role Conflict and Personality Factor N which is significant at .01 level. It shows that Personality Factors bright, conscientious, imaginative and shrewdness lead to increase the Role Conflict.

There are negative correlations between Role Conflict and Personality Factor F and $Q_4$ which are significant at .05 level. It shows that sober and relaxed women teachers belonging to joint family experience high Role Conflict.

Rest of the correlations between Role Conflict and Personality Factors A, C, E, H, I, L, O, $Q_1$, $Q_2$, and $Q_3$ are insignificant.

**Table 6.14. Coefficients of Correlation Between Role Conflict and Personality Factors of Women Teachers Having More Than Five Years of Teaching Experience**

| *Sr.No.* | *Personality Factors* | *Name of the Factor* | *'r' (Coefficient of Correlation)* |
|---|---|---|---|
| *1* | *2* | *3* | *4* |
| 1. | Reserved Vs. Outgoing | 'A' | –.1128 |
| 2. | Less Intelligent Vs. More Intelligent | 'B' | .0328 |
| 3. | Emotionally more Stable Vs. Less Stable | 'C' | –.0340 |
| 4. | Humble Vs. Assertive | 'E' | .1284 * |
| 5. | Sober Vs. Happy-go-lucky | 'F' | .1801 ** |
| 6. | Expedient Vs. Conscientious | 'G' | .0348 |
| 7. | Shy Vs. Venturesome | 'H' | .0801 |
| 8. | Tough Vs. Tender-minded | 'I' | .1391 * |
| 9. | Trusting Vs. Suspicious | 'L' | .0200 |
| 10. | Practical Vs. Imaginative | 'M' | –.0912 |
| 11. | Forthright Vs. Shrewd | 'N' | –.1444 * |
| 12. | Untroubled Vs. Troubled | 'O' | .0113 |
| 13. | Conservative Vs. Liberal | '$Q_1$' | .1239 |

*(Contd.)*

*(Contd.)*

| 1 | 2 | 3 | 4 |
|---|---|---|---|
| 14. | Group Dependent Vs. Self Sufficient | '$Q_2$' | .0711 |
| 15. | Undisciplined Vs. Controlled | '$Q_3$' | .0977 |
| 16. | Relaxed Vs. Tense | '$Q_4$' | –.1722 ** |

*Significant at .05 level. N = 220

**Significant at .01 level. df = 218

Table value at .05 level of significance = .1255.

Table value at .01 level of significance = .1645.

Table 6.14 reveals that Coefficient of correlation between Role Conflict and Personality Factor E, F, I, N, and $Q_4$ are significant.

There are positive correlations between Role Conflict and Personality Factor E and I which are significant at .05 level. There is also positive correlation between Role Conflict and Personality Factor F which is significant at .01 level. It shows that Personality Factors assertive, happy-go-lucky and tender-minded lead to increase the Role Conflict.

There are negative correlations between Role Conflict and Personality Factor N and $Q_4$ which are significant at .05 level and .01 level. It shows that forthright and relaxed women teachers experience high Role Conflict.

Rest of the correlations between Role Conflict and Personality Factors A, B, C, G, H, L, M, O, $Q_1$, $Q_2$ and $Q_3$ are insignificant.

**Table 6.15. Coefficients of Correlation Between Role Conflict and Personality Factors of Women Teachers Having Less Than Five Years of Teaching Experience**

| *Sr.No.* | *Personality Factors* | *Name of the Factor* | *'r' (Coefficient of Correlation)* |
|---|---|---|---|
| *1* | *2* | *3* | *4* |
| 1. | Reserved Vs. Outgoing | 'A' | .1495 * |

*(Contd.)*

*(Contd.)*

| *1* | *2* | *3* | *4* |
|---|---|---|---|
| 2. | Less Intelligent Vs. More Intelligent | 'B' | –.0379 |
| 3. | Emotionally more Stable Vs. Less Stable | 'C' | –.0840 |
| 4. | Humble Vs. Assertive | 'E' | .1573 * |
| 5. | Sober Vs. Happy-go-lucky | 'F' | .1811 * |
| 6. | Expedient Vs. Conscientious | 'G' | .1757 * |
| 7. | Shy Vs. Venturesome | 'H' | –.0175 |
| 8. | Tough Vs. Tender-minded | 'I' | .1334 |
| 9. | Trusting Vs. Suspicious | 'L' | –.1080 |
| 10. | Practical Vs. Imaginative | 'M' | .1723 * |
| 11. | Forthright Vs. Shrewd | 'N' | –.0817 |
| 12. | Untroubled Vs. Troubled | 'O' | .1112 |
| 13. | Conservative Vs. Liberal | '$Q_1$' | .1222 |
| 14. | Group Dependent Vs. Self Sufficient | '$Q_2$' | –.1621 * |
| 15. | Undisciplined Vs. Controlled | '$Q_3$' | –.0311 |
| 16. | Relaxed Vs. Tense | '$Q_4$' | .1665 * |

*Significant at .05 level. N = 140

df = 138

Table value at .05 level of significance = .1485.

Table value at .01 level of significance = .1945.

Table 6.15 reveals that the Coefficient of correlation between Role Conflict and Personality Factors A, E, F, G, M, $Q_2$ and $Q_4$ are significant.

There are positive correlations between Role Conflict and Personality Factors A, E, F, G, M, $Q_2$, and $Q_4$ which are significant at .05 level. This shows that Personality Factors outgoing, assertive, happy-go-lucky, conscientious, imaginative, self-sufficient and tense lead to increase Role Conflict.

Rest of the correlations between Role Conflict and Personality Factors B, C, H, I, L, N, O, $Q_1$ and $Q_3$ are insignificant.

**Table 6.16. Coefficients of Correlation Between Role Conflict and Personality Factors of Women Teachers Teaching in Government Schools**

| *Sr.No.* | *Personality Factors* | *Name of the Factor* | *'r' (Coefficient of Correlation)* |
|---|---|---|---|
| *1* | *2* | *3* | *4* |
| 1. | Reserved Vs. Outgoing | 'A' | –.0481 |
| 2. | Less Intelligent Vs. More Intelligent | 'B' | –.0231 |
| 3. | Emotionally more Stable Vs. Less Stable | 'C' | .1490 |
| 4. | Humble Vs. Assertive | 'E' | .2015 |
| 5. | Sober Vs. Happy-go-lucky | 'F' | .2514 * |
| 6. | Expedient Vs. Conscientious | 'G' | .2260 * |
| 7. | Shy Vs. Venturesome | 'H' | .2834 * |
| 8. | Tough Vs. Tender-minded | 'I' | .2934 ** |
| 9. | Trusting Vs. Suspicious | 'L' | –.2513 * |
| 10. | Practical Vs. Imaginative | 'M' | –.1424 |
| 11. | Forthright Vs. Shrewd | 'N' | .2341 * |
| 12. | Untroubled Vs. Troubled | 'O' | .1620 |
| 13. | Conservative Vs. Liberal | '$Q_1$' | .2530 * |
| 14. | Group Dependent Vs. Self Sufficient | '$Q_2$' | .1895 * |
| 15. | Undisciplined Vs. Controlled | '$Q_3$' | .3004 |
| 16. | Relaxed Vs. Tense | '$Q_4$' | –.0174 |

*Significant at .05 level. N = 80

**Significant at .01 level. df = 78

Table value at .05 level of significance = .225.

Table value at .01 level of significance = .292.

Table 6.16 reveals that the coefficient of correlation

between Role Conflict and Personality Factors F, G, H, I, L, N and $Q_1$ are significant.

There are positive correlations between Role Conflict and Personality Factors F, G,H, N and $Q_1$ which are significant at .05 level. There is also a positive correlation between Role Conflict and Personality Factor I which is significant at .01 level. This shows that Personality Factors happy-go-lucky, conscientious, venturesome, shrewdness, imaginative and tender-minded lead to increase the Role Conflict.

There is a negative correlation between Role Conflict and Personality Factor 'L' which is significant at .05 level. It shows that trusting women teachers teaching in government schools experience high Role Conflict.

Rest of the correlations between Role Conflict and Personality Factors A, B, C, E, M, O, $Q_2$, $Q_3$ and $Q_4$ are insignificant.

**Table 6.17. Coefficients of Correlation Between Role Conflict and Personality Factors of Women Teachers Teaching in Aided Schools**

| *Sr.No.* | *Personality Factors* | *Name of the Factor* | *'r' (Coefficient of Correlation)* |
|---|---|---|---|
| *1* | *2* | *3* | *4* |
| 1. | Reserved Vs. Outgoing | 'A' | –.1761 * |
| 2. | Less Intelligent Vs. More Intelligent | 'B' | –.1237 |
| 3. | Emotionally more Stable Vs. Less Stable | 'C' | –.0847 |
| 4. | Humble Vs. Assertive | 'E' | .0165 |
| 5. | Sober Vs. Happy-go-lucky | 'F' | –.1384 |
| 6. | Expedient Vs. Conscientious | 'G' | –.1851 * |
| 7. | Shy Vs. Venturesome | 'H' | .1223 |
| 8. | Tough Vs. Tender-minded | 'I' | .1960 * |
| 9. | Trusting Vs. Suspicious | 'L' | .2330 * |
| 10. | Practical Vs. Imaginative | 'M' | .1790 * |

*(Contd.)*

*(Contd.)*

| *1* | *2* | *3* | *4* |
|---|---|---|---|
| 11. | Forthright Vs. Shrewd | 'N' | .1680 |
| 12. | Untroubled Vs. Troubled | 'O' | .3102 ** |
| 13. | Conservative Vs. Liberal | '$Q_1$' | –.2101 * |
| 14. | Group Dependent Vs. Self Sufficient | '$Q_2$' | .1321 |
| 15. | Undisciplined Vs. Controlled | '$Q_3$' | .3219 ** |
| 16. | Relaxed Vs. Tense | '$Q_4$' | .1883 * |

*Significant at .05 level. N = 130

**Significant at .01 level. df = 128

Table value at .05 level of significance = .1665.

Table value at .01 level of significance = .2925.

Table 6.17 reveals that the coefficients of correlation between Role Conflict and Personality Factors A, G, I, L, M, N, $O_1$, $Q_3$ and $Q_4$ are significant.

There are positive correlation between Role Conflict and Personality Factors I, L, M, N, and $Q_4$ which are significant at .05 level. The correlations between Role Conflict and Personality Factors O and $Q_3$ are also positive and significant at .01 level. This shows that the Personality Factors tender-minded, suspicious, imaginative, shrewdness, tense, apprehensive and controlled lead to increase the Role Conflict.

There are negative correlations between Role Conflict and Personality Factors A, G, and $Q_1$ which are significant at .05 level. It shows that reserved, expedient, and conservative women teachers teaching in aided schools experience high Role Conflict.

Rest of the correlations between Role Conflict and Personality Factors B, C, E, F, H and $Q_2$ are insignificant.

**Table 6.18. Coefficients of Correlation Between Role Conflict and Personality Factors of Women Teachers Teaching in Private Schools**

| *Sr.No.* | *Personality Factors* | *Name of the Factor* | *'r' (Coefficient of Correlation)* |
|---|---|---|---|
| *1* | *2* | *3* | *4* |
| 1. | Reserved Vs. Outgoing | 'A' | .0624 |
| 2. | Less Intelligent Vs. More Intelligent | 'B' | –.2061** |
| 3. | Emotionally more Stable Vs. Less Stable | 'C' | .1276 |
| 4. | Humble Vs. Assertive | 'E' | –.1334 |
| 5. | Sober Vs. Happy-go-lucky | 'F' | .1494* |
| 6. | Expedient Vs. Conscientious | 'G' | .1834* |
| 7. | Shy Vs. Venturesome | 'H' | .1491* |
| 8. | Tough Vs. Tender-minded | 'I' | .0981 |
| 9. | Trusting Vs. Suspicious | 'L' | –.1671* |
| 10. | Practical Vs. Imaginative | 'M' | .1475 |
| 11. | Forthright Vs. Shrewd | 'N' | .0850 |
| 12. | Untroubled Vs. Troubled | 'O' | .0312 |
| 13. | Conservative Vs. Liberal | '$Q_1$' | .1834* |
| 14. | Group Dependent Vs. Self Sufficient | '$Q_2$' | .2076** |
| 15. | Undisciplined Vs. Controlled | '$Q_3$' | .1078 |
| 16. | Relaxed Vs. Tense | '$Q_4$' | .1947** |

*Significant at .05 level. N = 140

**Significant at .01 level. df = 148

Table value at .05 level of significance = .1485.

Table value at .01 level of significance = .1945.

Table 6.18 reveals that coefficient of correlation between Role Conflict and Personality Factors B, F, G, H, L, $Q_1$, $Q_2$ and $Q_4$ are significant.

There are positive correlations between Role Conflict and Personality Factors F, G, H, and $Q_1$ which are significant at

.05 level. There are also positive correlations between Role Conflict and Personality Factors $Q_2$ and $Q_4$ which are significant at .01 level. This shows that Personality Factors happy-go-lucky, conscientious, venturesome, imaginative, self-sufficient and tense lead to increase Role Conflict.

There are negative correlations between Role Conflict and Personality Factors B and L which are significant at .01 level and .05 level respectively. It shows that dull* and trusting women teachers teaching in private schools experience high Role Conflict.

Rest of the correlations between Rest Conflict and Personality Factors A, C, E, I, M, N, O and $Q_3$ are insignificant.

**Table 6.19. Coefficients of Correlation Between Role Conflict and Personality Factors of Women Teachers Teaching in Girls Schools**

| *Sr.No.* | *Personality Factors* | *Name of the Factor* | *'r' (Coefficient of Correlation)* |
|---|---|---|---|
| *1* | *2* | *3* | *4* |
| 1. | Reserved Vs. Outgoing | 'A' | .1934 * |
| 2. | Less Intelligent Vs. More Intelligent | 'B' | .0134 |
| 3. | Emotionally more Stable Vs. Less Stable | 'C' | .0285 |
| 4. | Humble Vs. Assertive | 'E' | .1856 * |
| 5. | Sober Vs. Happy-go-lucky | 'F' | .0124 |
| 6. | Expedient Vs. Conscientious | 'G' | .1764 |
| 7. | Shy Vs. Venturesome | 'H' | .1921 * |
| 8. | Tough Vs. Tender-minded | 'I' | –.1890 * |
| 9. | Trusting Vs. Suspicious | 'L' | –.2011 * |
| 10. | Practical Vs. Imaginative | 'M' | .1955 * |
| 11. | Forthright Vs. Shrewd | 'N' | .0172 |
| 12. | Untroubled Vs. Troubled | 'O' | .1999 * |
| 13. | Conservative Vs. Liberal | '$Q_1$' | .2332 ** |

*(Contd.)*

*means less intelligent.

*(Contd.)*

| 1 | 2 | 3 | 4 |
|---|---|---|---|
| 14. | Group Dependent Vs. Self Sufficient | '$Q_2$' | .1172 |
| 15. | Undisciplined Vs. Controlled | '$Q_3$' | .0342 |
| 16. | Relaxed Vs. Tense | '$Q_4$' | .1872 * |

*Significant at .05 level. N = 105

**Significant at .01 level. df = 103

Table value at .05 level of significance = .1845.

Table value at .01 level of significance = .2267.

Table 6.19 indicates that coefficients of correlation between Role Conflict and Personality Factors A, E, H, I, L, M, O, $Q_1$ and $Q_4$ are significant.

There are positive correlation between Role Conflict and Personality Factors A, E, H, M, O and $Q_4$ which are significant at .05 level. There is also a positive correlation between Role Conflict and Personality Factor $Q_1$ which is significant at .01 level. It shows that Personality Factors outgoing, assertive, venturesome, imaginative, apprehensive tense and liberal lead to increase Role Conflict.

There are negative correlations between Role Conflict and Personality Factors I and L which are significant at .05 level. It shows that tough minded and trusting women teachers teaching in girls schools experience high Role Conflict.

Rest of the correlations between Role Conflict and Personality Factors B, C, F, G, N, $Q_2$ and $Q_3$ are insignificant.

**Table 6.20. Coefficients of Correlation Between Role Conflict and Personality Factors of Women Teachers Teaching in Boys Schools**

| *Sr.No.* | *Personality Factors* | *Name of the Factor* | *'r' (Coefficient of Correlation)* |
|---|---|---|---|
| *1* | *2* | *3* | *4* |
| 1. | Reserved Vs. Outgoing | 'A' | .2001 * |

*(Contd.)*

*(Contd.)*

| *1* | *2* | *3* | *4* |
|---|---|---|---|
| 2. | Less Intelligent Vs. More Intelligent | 'B' | .1019 |
| 3. | Emotionally more Stable Vs. Less Stable | 'C' | .0662 |
| 4. | Humble Vs. Assertive | 'E' | .1884 * |
| 5. | Sober Vs. Happy-go-lucky | 'F' | –.1008 |
| 6. | Expedient Vs. Conscientious | 'G' | .1921 * |
| 7. | Shy Vs. Venturesome | 'H' | .0223 |
| 8. | Tough Vs. Tender-minded | 'I' | .1998 * |
| 9. | Trusting Vs. Suspicious | 'L' | –.1885 * |
| 10. | Practical Vs. Imaginative | 'M' | .1992 * |
| 11. | Forthright Vs. Shrewd | 'N' | –.0172 |
| 12. | Untroubled Vs. Troubled | 'O' | .1112 |
| 13. | Conservative Vs. Liberal | '$Q_1$' | .0372 |
| 14. | Group Dependent Vs. Self Sufficient | '$Q_2$' | .1890 * |
| 15. | Undisciplined Vs. Controlled | '$Q_3$' | .0332 |
| 16. | Relaxed Vs. Tense | '$Q_4$' | .1923 * |

*Significant at .05 level. N = 120

df = 118

Table value at .05 level of significance = .1845.

Table value at .01 level of significance = .2267.

Table 6.20. reveals that the coefficient of correlation between Role Conflict and Personality Factors A, E, G, I, L, M, $Q_2$ and $Q_4$ are significant.

There are positive correlations between Role Conflict and Personality Factors A, E, G, I, M, $Q_2$ and $Q_4$ which are significant at .05 level. It shows that Personality Factors outgoing, assertive, conscientious, tender minded, imaginative, self sufficient and tense lead to increase the Role Conflict.

There is a negative correlation between Role Conflict and Personality Factor 'L' which is significant at .05 level. It shows that trusting women teachers teaching in boys schools experience high Role Conflict.

Rest of the correlations between Role Conflict and Personality Factors B, C, F, H, N, O, $Q_1$ and $Q_3$ are insignificant.

**Table 6.21. Coefficients of Correlation Between Role Conflict and Personality Factors of Women Teachers Teaching in Co-educational Schools**

| *Sr.No.* | *Personality Factors* | *Name of the Factor* | *'r' (Coefficient of Correlations)* |
|---|---|---|---|
| *1* | *2* | *3* | *4* |
| 1. | Reserved Vs. Outgoing | 'A' | .1563 * |
| 2. | Less Intelligent Vs. More Intelligent | 'B' | .0312 |
| 3. | Emotionally more Stable Vs. Less Stable | 'C' | .0666 |
| 4. | Humble Vs. Assertive | 'E' | .0120 |
| 5. | Sober Vs. Happy-go-lucky | 'F' | .1032 |
| 6. | Expedient Vs. Conscientious | 'G' | .1601 * |
| 7. | Shy Vs. Venturesome | 'H' | .0320 |
| 8. | Tough Vs. Tender-minded | 'I' | .1545 * |
| 9. | Trusting Vs. Suspicious | 'L' | .0121 |
| 10. | Practical Vs. Imaginative | 'M' | .0781 |
| 11. | Forthright Vs. Shrewd | 'N' | .1777 * |
| 12. | Untroubled Vs. Troubled | 'O' | .1231 |
| 13. | Conservative Vs. Liberal | '$Q_1$' | .1652 * |
| 14. | Group Dependent Vs. Self Sufficient | '$Q_2$' | .1220 |
| 15. | Undisciplined Vs. Controlled | '$Q_3$' | .1268 |
| 16. | Relaxed Vs. Tense | '$Q_4$' | –.1980 ** |

*Significant at .05 level. N = 135

df = 133

Table value at .05 level of significance = .1485.

Table value at .01 level of significance = .1945.

Table 6.21 reveals that Coefficients of correlation between Role Conflict and Personality Factors A, G, I, N, $Q_1$ and $Q_4$ are significant.

There are positive correlations between Role Conflict and Personality Factors A, G, I, N, and $Q_1$ which are significant at .05 level. It shows that Personality Factors outgoing conscientious, tender minded, shrewdness and imaginative led to increase the Role Conflict.

There is a negative correlation between Role Conflict and Personality Factor $Q_4$ which is significant at .01 level. It shows that relaxed women teachers teaching in co-educational schools experience high Role Conflict.

Rest of the correlations between Role Conflict and Personality Factors B, C, E, F, H, L, M, O, $Q_2$ and $Q_3$ are insignificant.

## 6.3 COEFFICIENTS OF CORRELATION BETWEEN ROLE CONFLICT AND SOCIO-ECONOMIC STATUS OF WOMEN TEACHERS

Coefficients of correlation between Role Conflict and various categories of Socio-economic Status of women teachers were calculated in the following sections :

6.3.1 Correlation between Total Role Conflict and Socio-economic Status of women teachers.

6.3.2 Correlation between Inter Role Conflict and Socio-economic Status of women teachers.

6.3.3 Correlation between Intra Role Conflict and Socio-economic Status of women teachers.

6.3.4 Correlation between Family Role Conflict and Socio-economic Status of women teachers.

6.3.5 Correlation between Job Role Conflict and Socio Economic Status of women teachers.

The obtained results of coefficients of correlation are given in the table Number 6.22 to 6.26.

**Table 6.22. Coefficients of Correlation Between Total Role Conflict and Socio-economic Status Among Women Teachers**

| *Socio-Economic Status* | *N* | *'r' (Coefficients of Correlation)* | *df* |
|---|---|---|---|
| Upper Lower Class | 85 | –.2403 * | 83 |
| Upper Middle Class | 10 | –.0463 | 8 |
| Middle Class | 265 | –.1083 | 263 |
| Total | 360 | | |

*Significant at .05 level. N = 360

Table 6.22 indicates that the coefficient of correlation between Role Conflict and Socio-economic Status of upper lower class women teachers is negative which is significant at .05 level. It shows that lower the Socio-economic Status, higher will be the Role Conflict.

Correlations between Role Conflict and Socio-economic Status *i.e.* upper middle class and middle class are insignificant. It shows that there exists no significant relationship between Role Conflict and Socio-economic Status among women teachers of middle and upper middle classes.

**Table 6.23. Coefficients of Correlation Between Inter Role Conflict and Socio-economic Status of Women Teacher (N = 360)**

| *Socio-Economic Status* | *N* | *'r' (Coefficients of Correlation)* | *df* |
|---|---|---|---|
| Upper Lower Class | 85 | –.1028 | 83 |
| Upper Middle Class | 10 | –.0701 | 8 |
| Middle Class | 265 | –.1223 | 263 |
| Total | 360 | | |

Insignificant 'r'

Table 6.23 reveals that coefficients of correlation between Inter Role Conflict and Socio-economic Status of women teachers are insignificant. It shows that there exists no relationship between Inter Role Conflict and various categories of Socio-economic Status *i.e.* upper lower, upper middle and middle classes of women teachers.

**Table 6.24. Coefficients of Correlation Between Intra Role Conflict and Socio-economic Status of Women Teachers (N = 360)**

| *Socio-Economic Status* | *N* | *'r' (Coefficients of Correlation)* | *df* |
|---|---|---|---|
| Upper Lower Class | 85 | –.1736 | 83 |
| Upper Middle Class | 10 | –.1481 | 8 |
| Middle Class | 265 | –.0890 | 263 |
| Total | 360 | | |

Insignificant 'r'.

Table 6.24 indicates that the coefficients of correlation between Intra Role Conflict and various categories of Socio-economic Status are insignificant. It shows that there exists no relationship between Intra Role Conflict and Socio-economic status of women teachers.

**Table 6.25. Coefficients of Correlation Between Family Role Conflict and Socio-economic Status Among Women Teachers (N = 360)**

| *Socio-Economic Status* | *N* | *'r' (Coefficients of Correlation)* | *df* |
|---|---|---|---|
| Upper Lower Class | 85 | –.1898 | 83 |
| Upper Middle Class | 10 | –.0122 | 8 |
| Middle Class | 265 | –.1062 | 263 |
| Total | 360 | | |

Insignificant 'r'.

Table 6.25 reveals that the coefficients of correlation between family Role Conflict and various categories of Socio-economic Status are insignificant. It shows that there exists no relationship between family Role Conflict and Socio-economic Status of women teachers.

**Table 6.26. Coefficients of Correlation Between Job Role Conflict and Socio-economic Status Among Women Teachers (N = 360)**

| *Socio-Economic Status* | *N* | *'r' (Coefficients of Correlation)* | *df* |
|---|---|---|---|
| Upper Lower Class | 85 | –.0484 | 83 |
| Upper Middle Class | 10 | –.2158 | 8 |
| Middle Class | 265 | –.1145 | 263 |

Insignificant 'r'.

Table 6.26 indicates that the coefficients of correlation between job Role Conflict and various categories of Socio-economic Status are insignificant. It shows that there exists no relationship between job Role Conflict and Socio-economic Status of women teachers.

# 7 Comparison of Role Conflict and Demographic Variables

This Chapter proposes to investigate the significance of differences in Role Conflict among women teachers with respect to various demographic variables such as educational level, marital status, location of school, type of family, teaching experience, financing and management of school and type of school.

To realize the objectives of the study, the data were analysed with the help to t-test. The significance of t-test is judged at .05 and .01 level of significance. The analysis has been presented in the following sections.

7.1 Comparison of Role Conflict among women teachers with respect to demographic variables.

7.2a Comparison of Inter Role Conflict among women teachers with respect to demographic variables.

7.2b Comparison of Intra Role Conflict among women teachers with respect to demographic variables.

7.3 Comparison of Inter Role Conflict and Intra Role Conflict among women teachers with respect to demographic variables.

## 7.1 COMPARISON OF ROLE CONFLICT AMONG WOMEN TEACHERS WITH RESPECT TO DEMOGRAPHIC VARIABLES

A comparison of Role Conflict among women teachers was made with respect to educational level, marital status, location of the school, type of family, teaching experience, financing and management of school and type of school.

7.1.1 Comparison of Role Conflict in case of J.B.T. and B.Ed. women teachers.

7.1.2 Comparison of Role Conflict in case of married and unmarried women teachers.

7.1.3 Comparison of Role conflict in case of women teachers teaching in rural and urban schools.

7.1.4 Comparison of Role Conflict in case of women teachers with respect to the type of family they belong.

7.1.5 Comparison of Role Conflict in case of women teachers with respect to their teaching experience.

7.1.6 Comparison of Role Conflict in case of women teachers with respect to financing and management of schools.

7.1.7 Comparison of Role Conflict in case of women teachers with respect to the type of school.

The computed t-values with Means and Standard Deviations are shown in the Table Number 7.1 to 7.7.

**Table 7.1 Comparison of Role Conflict in Case of J.B.T. and B.Ed. Women Teachers**

| *Role Conflict* | *J.B.T.* $M_1$ | *($N_1$ = 170)* $SD_1$ | *B.Ed.* $M_2$ | *($N_2$ = 190)* $SD_2$ | *t* |
|---|---|---|---|---|---|
| Total Role Conflict | 103.335 | 16.718 | 102.905 | 17.431 | 0.238 |
| Inter Role Conflict | 55.941 | 48.026 | 54.316 | 12.942 | 0.112 |
| Intra Role Conflict | 47.971 | 8.422 | 45.700 | 7.978 | 2.366* |
| Family Role Conflict | 41.506 | 7.812 | 41.695 | 8.258 | 0.223 |
| Job Role Conflict | 43.306 | 8.340 | 42.489 | 8.379 | 0.928 |
| Social Role Conflict | 15.594 | 3.666 | 15.916 | 3.835 | 0.817 |
| Dual Role Conflict | 87.771 | 15.396 | 87.047 | 15.464 | 0.446 |

* Significant at .05 level.

Table 7.1 reveals that t-ratio in case of intra Role conflict being 2.366 is significant at .05 level of significance. It shows that J.B.T. women teachers experience more Intra Role Conflict than B.Ed. women teachers.

**Table 7.2 Comparison of Role Conflict in Case of Married and Unmarried Women Teachers**

| *Role Conflict* | *Unmarried* $(N_1 = 160)$ | | *Married* $(N_2 = 200)$ | | *t* |
|---|---|---|---|---|---|
| | $M_1$ | $SD_1$ | $M_2$ | $SD_2$ | |
| Total Role Conflict | 92.756 | 10.235 | 111.405 | 16.991 | 12.888 ** |
| Inter Role Conflict | 42.506 | 6.631 | 61.860 | 9.904 | 22.144 ** |
| Intra Role Conflict | 47.837 | 7.466 | 45.900 | 8.753 | 2.265 * |
| Family Role Conflict | 36.769 | 5.343 | 45.460 | 7.806 | 12.624 ** |
| Job Role Conflict | 39.594 | 5.855 | 45.570 | 9.101 | 7.564 ** |
| Social Role Conflict | 14.144 | 2.612 | 17.005 | 4.086 | 8.174 ** |
| Dual Role Conflict | 78.531 | 9.639 | 94.375 | 15.578 | 11.912 ** |

* Significant at .05 level.

** Significant at .01 level.

Table 7.2 reveals that t-ratio being 12.888, 22.144, 12.624, 7.564, 8.174, 11.912 are significant at .01 level. The t-value of 2.265 is also significant at .05 level. This shows that married and unmarried women teachers differ significantly on Role Conflict. It suggests that married women teachers experience more Role Conflict than their unmarried counterparts except intra Role Conflict.

**Table 7.3 Comparison of Role Conflict in Case of Women Teachers Teaching in Rural and Urban Schools**

| *Role Conflict* | *Rural* $(N_2 = 180)$ | | *Urban* $(N_2 = 180)$ | | *t* |
|---|---|---|---|---|---|
| | $M_1$ | $SD_1$ | $M_2$ | $SD_2$ | |
| Total Role Conflict | 99.167 | 15.502 | 107.050 | 17.703 | 4.504 ** |
| Inter Role Conflict | 51.228 | 13.060 | 55.828 | 12.939 | 3.382 ** |
| Intra Role Conflict | 45.350 | 7.666 | 48.194 | 8.597 | 3.345 ** |
| Family Role Conflict | 40.028 | 7.963 | 43.200 | 7.823 | 3.821 ** |
| Job Role Conflict | 41.267 | 7.806 | 44.489 | 8.609 | 4.296 ** |
| Social Role Conflict | 15.311 | 3.658 | 16.217 | 3.805 | 2.323 * |
| Dual Role Conflict | 83.894 | 14.177 | 90.883 | 15.847 | 4.423 ** |

* Significant at .05 level.

** Significant at .01 level.

Table 7.3 reveals that t-ratio being 4.504, 3.382, 3.345, 3.821, 4.296, 4.423 are significant at .01 level. The t-value of 2.323 is also significant at .05 level. This shows that women teachers working in rural and urban areas differ significantly on Role Conflict. It suggests that women teachers working in urban areas experience more Role Conflict than women teachers working in rural areas.

**Table 7.4 Comparison of Role Conflict in Case of Women Teachers with Respect to the Type of Family They Belong**

| *Role Conflict* | *Nuclear* ($N_1 = 160$) | | *Joint* ($N_2 = 200$) | | *t* |
|---|---|---|---|---|---|
| | $M_1$ | $S.D._1$ | $M_2$ | $S.D._2$ | |
| Total Role Conflict | 110.469 | 16.771 | 97.235 | 14.973 | 7.803 ** |
| Inter Role Conflict | 61.725 | 10.086 | 46.485 | 10.730 | 13.854 ** |
| Intra Role Conflict | 45.162 | 8.711 | 48.040 | 7.648 | 3.289 ** |
| Family Role Conflict | 45.250 | 7.987 | 38.675 | 6.863 | 8.270 ** |
| Job Role Conflict | 44.925 | 9.129 | 41.305 | 7.323 | 4.076 ** |
| Social Role Conflict | 17.019 | 4.121 | 14.705 | 3.135 | 5.933 ** |
| Dual Role Conflict | 93.550 | 15.307 | 82.360 | 13.618 | 7.266 ** |

** Significant at .01 level.

Table 7.4 reveals that t-ratio being 7.803, 13.854, 3.289, 8.270, 4.076, 5.933, and 7.266 are significant at .01 level. It shows that women teachers differ significantly with respect to the type of family they belong. It suggests that women teachers belonging to nuclear families experience more Role Conflict that women teachers belonging to joint families except on intra Role Conflict where as women teachers belonging to joint families experience more intra Role Conflict than women teachers belonging to nuclear families.

**Table 7.5 Comparison of Role Conflict in Case of Women Teachers with Respect to Their Teaching Experience**

| *Role Conflict* | *More than five years ($N_1$ = 140)* | | *Less than five years ($N_2$ = 220)* | | *t* |
|---|---|---|---|---|---|
| | $M_1$ | $S.D._1$ | $M_2$ | $S.D._2$ | |
| Total Role Conflict | 94.664 | 13.991 | 108.495 | 16.738 | 8.469 ** |
| Inter Role Conflict | 45.364 | 9.944 | 58.282 | 12.028 | 11.069 ** |
| Intra Role Conflict | 46.771 | 7.753 | 46.755 | 8.570 | 0.018 |
| Family Role Conflict | 37.543 | 6.358 | 44.177 | 7.990 | 8.728 ** |
| Job Role Conflict | 40.493 | 7.143 | 44.455 | 8.723 | 5.588 ** |
| Social Role Conflict | 14.279 | 2.874 | 16.659 | 3.999 | 6.556 ** |
| Dual Role Conflict | 80.143 | 12.752 | 91.909 | 15.241 | 7.702 ** |

** Significant at .01 level.

Table 7.5 reveals that t-ratio being 8.469, 11.069, 8.728, 5.588, 6.556, and 7.901 are significant at .01 level. This shows that women teachers having less than five years of teaching experience face more Role Conflict than their counterparts who have more than five years of teaching experience except in intra Role Conflict.

Table 7.6 reveals that t-ratio being 5.230, 3.819, 2.761, 5.357, 3.648 and 5.185 are significant at .01 level. The t-values of 2.076 is also significant at .05 level. This shows that women teachers teaching in aided schools experience more Role Conflict than their counterparts teaching in government schools.

It also reveals that t-ratio being 3.900, 3.542, 4.107, 7.022, and 3.550 are significant at .01 level. This shows that women teachers teaching in private schools experience more Role Conflict than their counterparts teaching in government schools (except in intra and family Role Conflict).

The table 7.6 also indicates that t-ratio being 2.660 is significant at .01 level of significance. This shows that women teachers teaching in aided schools experience more intra Role conflict than their counterparts teaching in private schools.

**Table 7.6 Comparison of Role Conflict in Case of Women Teachers with Respect to Financing and Management of Schools**

| *Role Conflict* | *Government* $N_1 = 80$ | | *Aided* $N_2 = 130$ | | *Private* $N_3 = 150$ | | *t-values* Govt. & Aided | Govt. & Private | Aided & Private |
|---|---|---|---|---|---|---|---|---|---|
| | $M_1$ | $SD_1$ | $M_2$ | $SD_2$ | $M_3$ | $SD_3$ | | | |
| Total Role Conflict | 96.000 | 12.742 | 106.592 | 16.409 | 103.880 | 18.540 | 5.230 ** | 3.900 ** | 1.488 |
| Inter Role Conflict | 49.037 | 10.413 | 59.200 | 54.215 | 54.740 | 13.719 | 2.076 * | 3.542 ** | 1.021 |
| Intra Role Conflict | 44.575 | 7.470 | 48.815 | 8.419 | 46.173 | 8.145 | 3.819 ** | 0.897 | 2.660** |
| Family Role Conflict | 40.300 | 6.707 | 43.092 | 7.747 | 42.180 | 8.700 | 2.761 ** | 1.821 | 0.928 |
| Job Role Conflict | 38.775 | 5.937 | 44.100 | 8.470 | 42.833 | 8.977 | 5.367 ** | 4.107 ** | 1.222 |
| Social Role Conflict | 14.462 | 3.514 | 16.308 | 3.685 | 15.993 | 3.789 | 3.648 ** | 7.022 ** | 1.583 |
| Dual Role Conflict | 81.313 | 11.746 | 90.438 | 15.125 | 87.987 | 16.490 | 5.185 ** | 3.550 ** | 1.304 |

* Significant at .05 level.

** Significant at .01 level.

**Table 7.7 Comparison of Role Conflict in Case of Women Teachers with Respect to the Type of School**

| *Role Conflict* | *Girls* | | *Boys* | | *Co-education* | | | | |
|---|---|---|---|---|---|---|---|---|---|
| | $N_1 = 105$ | | $N_2 = 120$ | | $N_3 = 135$ | | *t-values* | | |
| | $M_1$ | $SD_1$ | $M_2$ | $SD_2$ | $M_3$ | $SD_3$ | *Girls & Boys* | *Girls & Co-ed* | *Boys & Co-ed* |
| Total Role Conflict | 99.438 | 13.706 | 103.392 | 17.648 | 105.711 | 18.423 | 1.497 | 3.030 ** | 1.026 |
| Inter Role Conflict | 51.076 | 11.408 | 54.558 | 13.853 | 54.222 | 13.151 | 2.065 * | 1.991* | 0.198 |
| Intra Role Conflict | 45.857 | 7.344 | 46.500 | 7.578 | 46.489 | 8.835 | 0.645 | 0.607 | 0.010 |
| Family Role Conflict | 39.981 | 7.134 | 42.942 | 9.393 | 43.015 | 7.595 | 2.684 ** | 3.176 ** | 0.067 |
| Job Role Conflict | 41.886 | 6.173 | 42.567 | 8.169 | 43.333 | 9.263 | 0.687 | 1.449 | 0.684 |
| Social Role Conflict | 15.029 | 3.663 | 15.858 | 3.239 | 23.170 | 13.193 | 1.790 | 6.841 ** | 6.233** |
| Dual Role Conflict | 84.324 | 12.189 | 86.742 | 15.093 | 88.674 | 17.239 | 1.328 | 2.287* | 0.954 |

* Significant at .05 level.

** Significant at .01 level.

Table 7.7 reveals that t-ratio being 2.065 and 2.684 are significant at .05 level and .01 level of significance respectively. This shows that women teachers teaching in boys schools experience more inter Role Conflict and family Role Conflict than their counterparts teaching in Girls schools.

It also indicates that t-ratio being 3.030, 3.176 and 6.841 are significant at .01 level of significance. The t-values 1.991 and 2.287 are also significant at .05 level. This shows that women teachers teaching in co-educational schools differ significantly from their counterparts teaching in girls schools. The women teachers teaching in co-educational schools experience more Role Conflict than those teaching in girls schools except in intra Role Conflict and family Role Conflict.

The Table 7.7 also reveals that t-ratio being 6.233 is significant at .01 level of significance. This shows that women teachers teaching in co-educational schools and boys schools differ significantly on social Role Conflict. It makes clear that women teachers teaching in co-educational schools experience more social Role Conflict than those teaching in boys schools.

## 7.2 *(a)* COMPARISON OF INTER ROLE CONFLICT AMONG WOMEN TEACHERS WITH RESPECT TO DEMOGRAPHIC VARIABLES

A comparison of Inter Role Conflict among women teachers was made with respect to educational level, marital status, location of the school, type of family, teaching experience, financing and management of school and type of school.

7.2.1 Comparison of Inter family Role Conflict with respect to educational level, marital status, location of the school, type of family, teaching experience, financing and management of school and type of school.

7.2.2 Comparison of inter job Role Conflict with respect to educational level, marital status, location of the school, type of family, teaching experience, financing and management of school and type of school.

## 7.2 *(b)* COMPARISON OF INTRA ROLE CONFLICT AMONG WOMEN TEACHERS WITH RESPECT TO DEMOGRAPHIC VARIABLES

A comparison of Intra Role Conflict among women teachers was made with respect to educational level, marital status, location of the school, type of family, teaching experience, financing and management of school and type of school.

7.2.1 Comparison of Intra family Role Conflict with respect to educational level, marital status, location of the school, type of family, teaching experience, financing and management of school and type of school.

7.2.2 Comparison of intra job Role Conflict with respect to educational level, marital status, location of the school, type of family, teaching experience, financing and management of school and type of school.

The computed t-values with Means and Standard Deviations are shown in the Table Number 7.8 to 7.9.

**Educational Level**

Table 7.8 reveals that t-ratio being 2.059 is significant at .05 level of significance. This shows that J.B.T. and B.Ed. teachers differ significantly on intra family Role Conflict. It suggests that B.Ed. women teachers experience more intra family Role Conflict than that of J.B.T. women teachers.

**Marital Status**

Table 7.8 reveals that t-ratio being 17.988 is significant at .01 level of significance. This shows that married and unmarried women teachers differ significantly on inter family Role Conflict. It leads to the inference that married women teachers experience more inter family Role Conflict than their unmarried counterparts.

**Location of the School**

Table 7.8 reveals that t-ratio being 3.697 is significant at .01 level of significance. This shows that women teachers teaching

**Table 7.8 Comparison of Inter Family Role Conflict and Intra Family Role Conflict Among Women Teachers**

| *Sr. No.* | Inter Family Role Conflict | | | | Intra Family Role Conflict | | |
|---|---|---|---|---|---|---|---|
| | *N* | *Mean* | *S.D.* | *t-values* | *Mean* | *S.D.* | *t-values* |
| *1* | *2* | *3* | *4* | *5* | *6* | *7* | *8* |
| **I. Educational level** | | | | | | | |
| *(i)* J.B.T. | 170 | 21.600 | 6.345 | | 19.753 | 3.737 | |
| | | | | 0.768 | | | 2.059* |
| *(ii)* B.Ed. | 190 | 21.116 | 5.599 | | 20.589 | 3.978 | |
| **II. Marital Status** | | | | | | | |
| *(i)* Married | 200 | 25.775 | 4.476 | | 19.604 | 3.981 | |
| | | | | 17.988** | | | 1.762 |
| *(ii)* Unmarried | 160 | 16.187 | 2.444 | | 20.556 | 3.250 | |
| **III. Location** | | | | | | | |
| *(i)* Rural | 180 | 20.300 | 5.776 | | 19.711 | 3.950 | |
| | | | | 3.697** | | | 1.021 |
| *(ii)* Urban | 180 | 22.589 | 5.966 | | 19.283 | 4.023 | |
| **IV. Type of Family** | | | | | | | |
| *(i)* Married | 80 | 26.400 | 4.883 | | 18.575 | 3.622 | |
| | | | | 17.103** | | | 3.292** |

*(Contd.)*

*(Contd.)*

| 1 | 2 | 3 | 4 | 5 | 6 | 7 | 8 |
|---|---|---|---|---|---|---|---|
| *(ii)* Unmarried | 80 | 16.138 | 2.428 | | 20.287 | 2.942 | |
| **B. Joint** | | | | | | | |
| *(i)* Married | 120 | 25.150 | 4.070 | 19.376** | 20.633 | 4.340 | 0.342 |
| *(ii)* Unmarried | 80 | 16.237 | 2.461 | | 20.825 | 3.559 | |
| **V. Teaching Experience** | | | | | | | |
| *(i)* More than five years | 220 | 24.882 | 4.924 | 22.684** | 19.923 | 4.133 | 1.436 |
| *(ii)* Less than five years | 140 | 16.043 | 2.487 | | 20.486 | 3.268 | |
| **VI. Financing and Management of School** | | | | | | | |
| A. *(i)* Govt. | 80 | 16.138 | 2.428 | 6.186** | 20.287 | 2.942 | 1.077 |
| *(ii)* Aided | 130 | 19.231 | 4.912 | | 20.815 | 4.147 | |
| B. *(i)* Govt. | 80 | 16.138 | 2.428 | 22.344** | 20.287 | 2.942 | 1.793 |
| *(ii)* Private | 150 | 26.193 | 4.475 | | 19.480 | 3.852 | |

*(Contd.)*

*(Contd.)*

| *1* | *2* | *3* | *4* | *5* | *6* | *7* | *8* |
|---|---|---|---|---|---|---|---|
| C. *(i)* Aided | 130 | 19.231 | 4.912 | | 20.815 | 4.147 | |
| | | | | 12.432** | | | 2.782** |
| *(ii)* Private | 150 | 26.193 | 4.750 | | 19.480 | 3.852 | |
| **VII. Type of School** | | | | | | | |
| A. *(i)* Girls | 105 | 16.057 | 2.518 | | 20.345 | 3.067 | |
| | | | | 8.940** | | | 1.302 |
| B. *(ii)* Boys | 120 | 20.708 | 5.057 | | 20.983 | 4.317 | |
| B. *(i)* Girls | 105 | 16.057 | 2.518 | | 20.345 | 3.067 | |
| | | | | 21.770** | | | 2.568** |
| *(ii)* Co-educational | 135 | 26.289 | 4.611 | | 19.215 | 3.719 | |
| C. *(i)* Boys | 120 | 20.708 | 5.057 | | 20.983 | 4.137 | |
| | | | | 9.149** | | | 3.843** |
| *(ii)* Co-educational | 135 | 26.289 | 4.611 | | 19.215 | 3.719 | |

* Significant at .05 level.

** Significant at .01 level.

in rural and urban schools differ significantly on inter family Role Conflict. It indicates that women teachers teaching in urban schools experience more inter family Role Conflict than their counterparts teaching in rural schools.

**Type of Family**

Table 7.8 reveals that t-ratio being 17.103 and 3.292 are significant at .01 level of significance. This shows that married and unmarried women teachers differ significantly on inter family Role Conflict and intra family Role Conflict belonging to nuclear families. It suggests that married women teachers experience more inter family Role Conflict than unmarried women teachers living in nuclear families and unmarried women teachers experience more intra family Role Conflict than married women teachers living in nuclear families.

It also reveals that t-ratio being 19.376 is significant at .01 level of significance. This shows that both married and unmarried women teachers living in joint families differ significantly on inter family Role Conflict. It suggests that married women teachers experience more inter family Role Conflict than their unmarried counterparts living in joint families.

**Teaching Experience**

Table 7.8 reveals that t-ratio being 22.684 is significant at .01 level of significance. It shows that women teachers having more than five years of teaching experience and women teachers having less than five years of teaching experience differ significantly on inter family Role Conflict. It suggests that women teachers having more than five years of teaching experience, experience more inter family Role Conflict than those of shows that women teachers teaching in girls school, boys school and co-educational schools differ significantly on inter family Role Conflict.

It also indicates that women teachers teaching in boys schools, experience more inter family Role Conflict than their counterparts teaching in girls schools. On the other hand, it indicates that women teachers teaching in co-educational

**Table 7.9 Comparison of Inter Job Role Conflict and Intra Job Role Conflict Among Women Teachers**

| *Sr. No.* | | *Inter Job Role Conflict* | | | *Intra Job Role Conflict* | | |
|---|---|---|---|---|---|---|---|
| | *N* | *Mean* | *S.D.* | *t-values* | *Mean* | *S.D.* | *t-values* |
| *1* | *2* | *3* | *4* | *5* | *6* | *7* | *8* |
| **I. Educational Level** | | | | | | | |
| (*i*) J.B.T. | 170 | 18.300 | 3.263 | | 24.706 | 5.961 | |
| | | | | 1.152 | | | 0.088 |
| (*ii*) B.Ed. | 190 | 17.868 | 3.884 | | 24.768 | 5.898 | |
| **II. Marital Status** | | | | | | | |
| (*i*) Married | 200 | 18.606 | 4.028 | | 26.998 | 6.264 | |
| | | | | 1.193 | | | 6.740** |
| (*ii*) Unmarried | 160 | 17.625 | 2.691 | | 21.943 | 3.586 | |
| **III. Location** | | | | | | | |
| (*i*) Rural | 180 | 18.028 | 3.622 | | 23.444 | 5.226 | |
| | | | | 3.920 ** | | | 4.254** |
| (*ii*) Urban | 180 | 19.517 | 3.588 | | 26.039 | 6.371 | |
| **IV. Type of Family Nuclear** | | | | | | | |
| (*i*) Marrieds | 80 | 18.987 | 3.600 | | 26.188 | 6.124 | |
| | | | | 2.025 * | | | 6.036** |

*(Contd.)*

(Contd.)

| 1 | 2 | 3 | 4 | 5 | 6 | 7 | 8 |
|---|---|---|---|---|---|---|---|
| (ii) Unmarrieds | 80 | 17.950 | 2.846 | | 21.600 | 3.101 | |
| **B. Joint** | | | | | | | |
| (i) Married | 120 | 18.225 | 4.456 | | 27.808 | 6.405 | |
| | | | | 2.040 * | | | 7.460** |
| (ii) Unmarried | 80 | 17.300 | 2.537 | | 22.287 | 4.072 | |
| **V. Teaching Experience** | | | | | | | |
| (i) More than five years | 220 | 18.436 | 4.052 | | 26.627 | 6.316 | |
| | | | | 2.169 * | | | 9.000** |
| (ii) Less than five years | 140 | 17.664 | 2.701 | | 21.893 | 3.664 | |
| **VI. Financing and Management of the School** | | | | | | | |
| A. (i) Govt. | 80 | 17.950 | 2.846 | | 21.600 | 3.101 | |
| | | | | 0.277 | | | 3.168** |
| (ii) Aided | 130 | 18.077 | 3.749 | | 23.392 | 5.100 | |
| B. (i) Govt. | 80 | 17.950 | 2.846 | | 21.600 | 3.101 | |
| | | | | 0.710 | | | 9.935** |
| (ii) Private | 150 | 18.267 | 3.847 | | 27.760 | 6.344 | |

(Contd.)

*(Contd.)*

| *1* | *2* | *3* | *4* | *5* | *6* | *7* | *8* |
|---|---|---|---|---|---|---|---|
| C. *(i)* Aided | 130 | 18.077 | 3.749 | | 23.392 | 5.100 | |
| | | | | 0.422 | | | 6.519** |
| *(ii)* Private | 150 | 18.267 | 3.847 | | 27.760 | 6.344 | |
| **VII. Type of School** | | | | | | | |
| A. *(i)* Girls | 105 | 17.705 | 2.725 | | 21.590 | 3.371 | |
| | | | | 0.207 | | | 4.680** |
| *(ii)* Boys | 120 | 17.800 | 4.053 | | 24.258 | 5.165 | |
| B. *(i)* Girls | 105 | 17.705 | 2.725 | | 21.590 | 3.371 | |
| | | | | 0.252 | | | 4.806** |
| *(ii)* Co-educational | 135 | 18.748 | 3.717 | | 27.815 | 6.577 | |
| C. *(i)* Boys | 120 | 17.800 | 4.053 | | 24.258 | 5.165 | |
| | | | | 1.930 | | | 4.839** |
| *(ii)* Co-educational | 135 | 18.748 | 3.717 | | 27.815 | 6.577 | |

* Significant at .05 level.

** Significant at .01 level.

schools experience more inter family Role Conflict than their counterparts teaching in girls schools and boys schools. Women teachers teaching in girls schools and boys schools experience more intra family Role Conflict than their counterparts teaching in co-educational schools.

**Educational Level**

Table 7.9 reveals that t-ratio being 1.152 and 0.088 are insignificant. This shows that J.B.T. and B.Ed. women teachers do not differ significantly on inter job Role Conflict and intra job Role Conflict.

**Marital Status**

Table 7.9 reveals that t-ratio being 6.740 is significant at .01 level of significant. This shows that married and unmarried women teachers differ significantly on intra job Role Conflict. It suggests that married women teachers experience more intra job Role Conflict than their unmarried counterparts.

**Location of the School**

Table 7.9 reveals that t-ratio being 3.920 and 4.254 are significant at .01 level of significance. This shows that women teachers teaching in rural and urban areas differ significantly on inter job Role Conflict and intra job Role Conflict. It suggests that women teachers teaching in urban areas experience more inter and intra job Role Conflict than women teachers teaching in rural areas.

**Type of Family**

Table 7.9 reveais that t-ratio being 2.025, and 2.040 are significant at .05 level of significance. It shows that married and unmarried women teachers living in nuclear families or joint families differ significantly on inter job Role Conflict. It indicates that married women teachers living in nuclear families experience more inter job Role Conflict than their unmarried counterparts.

It also reveals that t-ratio being 6.036 and 7.460 are significant at .01 level of significance. It shows that married and unmarried women teachers differ significantly on intra job Role Conflict living in nuclear and joint families. It suggests that married women teachers have more intra job Role Conflict than their unmarried counterparts.

**Teaching Experience**

Table 7.9 reveals that t-ratio being 2.169 and 9.000 are significant at .05 level and .01 level of significance respectively. This shows that women teachers having more than five years of teaching experience and less than five years of teaching experience differ significantly on inter job Role Conflict and intra Job Role Conflict. It suggests that women teachers having more than five years of teaching experience have to face more inter job Role Conflict and intra job Role Conflict than those of having less than five years of teaching experience.

**Financing and Management of School**

Table 7.9 reveals that t-ratio being 3.168, 9.935 and 6.519 are significant at .01 level. This shows that women teachers teaching in government, aided and private schools differ significantly on intra job Role Conflict. This suggests that women teachers teaching in aided and private schools experience more intra job Role Conflict than their counterparts teaching in government schools. Further, it also reveals that women teachers teaching in private schools experience more intra job Role Conflict than those teaching in government and aided schools.

**Type of School**

Table 7.9 reveals that t-ratio being 4.680, 4.806 and 4.839 are significant at .01 level of significance. This shows that women teachers teaching in girls schools, boys schools and co-educational schools differ significantly on intra job Role Conflict. It indicates that women teachers teaching in boys and co-educational schools face more intra job Role conflict than their counterparts teaching in girls schools. Further, it also reveals that women teachers teaching in co-educational schools face more intra job Role Conflict than those women teachers teaching in girls and boys schools.

## 7.3 COMPARISON BETWEEN INTER ROLE CONFLICT AND INTRA ROLE CONFLICT WITH RESPECT TO DEMOGRAPHIC VARIABLES

A comparison between inter Role Conflict and intra Role Conflict was made with respect to educational level marital status, location of the school, type of family, teaching experience, financing and management of school and type of school.

7.3.1 Comparison between inter family Role Conflict and intra family Role Conflict with respect to educational level, marital status, location of the school type of family, teaching experience, financing and management of school and type of school.

7.3.2 Comparison between inter job Role Conflict and intra job Role Conflict with respect to educational level, marital status, location of the school, type of family, teaching experience, financing and management of school and type of school.

The computed t-values with Means and Standard Deviations are shown in the Table Number 7.10 to 7.11.

**Interpretation**

Educational Level

Table 7.10 reveals that t-ratio being 3.261 is significant at .01 level of significance. This shows that J.B.T. women teachers differ significantly on inter family Role Conflict and intra family Role Conflict. It also indicates that J.B.T. women teachers experience more inter family Role Conflict than intra family Role Conflict.

**Marital Status**

Table 7.10 reveals that t-ratio being 14.692 and 13.653 are significant at .01 level of significance. This shows that married and unmarried women teachers differ significantly on inter family Role Conflict and intra family Role Conflict. Further, it also indicates that married women teachers experience more inter family Role Conflict than intra family Role Conflict.

**Table 7.10. Comparison Between Inter Family Role Conflict and Intra Job Role Conflict Among Women Teachers (N = 360)**

| *Sr. No.* | *Correlates of Role Conflict* | *N* | *Inter Family Role Conflict* | | *Vs.* | *Intra Family Role Conflict* | | |
|---|---|---|---|---|---|---|---|---|
| | | | *Mean* ($M_1$) | *S.D.* ($\sigma_1$) | — | *Mean* ($M_2$) | *S.D.* ($\sigma_2$) | *t-values* |
| *1* | *2* | *3* | *4* | *5* | *6* | *7* | *8* | *9* |
| **I. Educational Level** | | | | | | | | |
| | *(i)* J.B.T. | 170 | 21.600 | 6.345 | — | 19.753 | 3.737 | 3.261** |
| | *(ii)* B.Ed. | 190 | 21.116 | 5.599 | — | 20.589 | 3.978 | 1.054 |
| **II. Marital Status** | | | | | | | | |
| | *(i)* Married | 200 | 25.775 | 4.476 | — | 19.604 | 3.981 | 14.692** |
| | *(ii)* Unmarried | 160 | 16.187 | 2.444 | — | 20.556 | 3.250 | 13.653** |
| **III. Location** | | | | | | | | |
| | *(i)* Rural | 180 | 20.300 | 5.776 | — | 19.711 | 3.950 | 1.126** |
| | *(ii)* Urban | 180 | 22.589 | 5.966 | — | 19.283 | 4.023 | 6.146** |
| **IV. Type of Family** | | | | | | | | |
| | **A. Married** | | | | | | | |
| | *(i)* Nuclear | 80 | 26.400 | 4.883 | — | 18.575 | 3.622 | 11.440** |
| | *(ii)* Joint | 120 | 25.150 | 4.070 | — | 20.633 | 3.340 | 8.282** |

*(Contd.)*

*(Contd.)*

| 1 | 2 | 3 | 4 | 5 | 6 | 7 | 8 | 9 |
|---|---|---|---|---|---|---|---|---|
| | **B. Unmarried** | | | | | | | |
| | *(i)* Nuclear | 80 | 16.138 | 2.428 | — | 20.287 | 2.942 | 9.671** |
| | *(ii)* Joint | 80 | 16.237 | 2.461 | — | 20.825 | 3.559 | 9.423** |
| **V. Teaching Experience** | | | | | | | | |
| | *(i)* More than five years | 220 | 24.822 | 4.924 | — | 19.923 | 4.133 | 11.415** |
| | *(ii)* Less than five years | 140 | 16.043 | 2.487 | — | 20.486 | 3.268 | 12.756** |
| **VI. Financing and Management of School** | | | | | | | | |
| | *(i)* Government | 80 | 16.138 | 2.428 | — | 20.287 | 2.942 | 9.671** |
| | *(ii)* Aided | 130 | 19.231 | 4.912 | — | 20.815 | 4.147 | 2.780** |
| | *(iii)* Private | 150 | 26.193 | 4.475 | — | 19.480 | 3.852 | 13.880** |
| **VII. Type of School** | | | | | | | | |
| | *(i)* Girls School | 105 | 16.057 | 2.518 | — | 20.345 | 3.067 | 11.014** |
| | *(ii)* Boys School | 120 | 20.708 | 5.057 | — | 20.983 | 4.317 | 0.451** |
| | *(iii)* Co-educational | 135 | 26.289 | 4.611 | — | 19.215 | 3.719 | 13.825** |

**Significant at .01 level.

Whereas unmarried women teachers experience more intra family Role Conflict than inter family Role Conflict.

**Location of School**

Table 7.10 reveals that t-ratio being 6.146 is significant at .01 level of significance. This shows that women teachers teaching in urban schools differ significantly on inter family Role Conflict and intra family Role Conflict. It also suggests that women teachers teaching in urban schools experience more inter family Role Conflict than intra family Role Conflict.

**IV. Type of Family**

Table 7.10 reveals that t-ratio being 11.440 and 8.282 are significant at .01 level of significance. This shows that married women teachers living in nuclear and joint families differ significantly on inter family Role Conflict and intra family Role Conflict. It indicates that married women teachers face more inter family Role Conflict than intra Family Role Conflict living in nuclear families as well as joint families.

The t-ratio being 9.671 and 9.423 are significant at .01 level of significance. This shows that unmarried women teachers differ significantly on inter family Role Conflict and intra family Role Conflict. Further, it indicates that unmarried women teachers living in nuclear and joint families experience more intra Family role conflict than inter family role conflict.

**V. Teaching Experience**

Table 7.10 reveals that t-ratio being 11.415 and 12.756 are significant at .01 level of significance. This shows that women teachers having more than five years of teaching experience and less than five years of teaching experience differ significantly on inter family Role Conflict and intra family Role Conflict. It also indicates that women teachers having more than five years of teaching experience are prone to inter family Role Conflict than intra family Role Conflict. Whereas women teachers having less than five years of teaching experience are prone to more intra family Role Conflict.

**VI. Financing and Management of School**

Table 7.10 reveals that t-ratio being 9.671, 2.780 and 13.880 are significant at .01 level of significance. This shows that women teachers teaching in government schools, aided schools and private schools differ significantly on inter family Role Conflict and intra family Role Conflict. Further, it indicates that women teachers teaching in government schools and aided schools experience more intra family Role Conflict than inter family Role Conflict whereas women teachers teaching in private schools experience more inter family Role Conflict than intra family Role Conflict.

**VII. Type of School**

Table 7.10 reveals that t-ratio being 11.014 and 13.825 are significant at .01 level of significance. This shows that women teachers teaching in girls schools and co-educational schools differ significantly on inter family Role Conflict and intra family Role Conflict. It also indicates that women teachers in girls schools experience more intra family Role Conflict than inter family Role Conflict. Whereas women teachers teaching in coeducational schools experience more inter family Role Conflict than intra family Role Conflict.

**I. Educational Level**

Table 7.11 reveals that t-ratio being 12.254 and 13.432 are significant at .01 level of significance. This shows that J.B.T. and B.Ed women teachers differ significantly on inter job Role Conflict and intra job Role Conflict. It also indicates that J.B.T. and B.Ed. women teachers have more intra job Role Conflict than inter job Role Conflict.

**II. Marital Status**

Table 7.11 reveals that t-ratio being 16.138 and 12.337 are significant at .01 level of significance. This shows that married and unmarried women teachers differ significantly on inter job Role Conflict and intra job Role Conflict. It indicates that both married and unmarried women teachers experience more intra job Role Conflict than inter job Role Conflict.

**III. Location of the School**

Table 7.11 reveals that t-ratio being 11.398 and 11.934 are significant at .01 level of significance. This shows that women teachers teaching in rural areas and urban areas differ significantly on inter job Role Conflict and intra job Role

**Table 7.11. Comparison Between Inter Job Role Conflict and Intra Job Role Conflict Among Women Teachers**

| *Sr. No.* | *N* | *Inter Job Role Conflict* | | *Intra Job Role Conflict* | | *t-values* |
|---|---|---|---|---|---|---|
| | | *Mean* ($M_1$) | *S.D.* ($\sigma_1$) | *Mean* ($M_2$) | *S.D.* ($\sigma_2$) | |
| *1* | *2* | *3* | *4* | *5* | *6* | *7* |
| **I. Educational Level** | | | | | | |
| *(i)* J.B.T. | 170 | 18.300 | 3.263 | 24.706 | 5.961 | 12.254** |
| *(ii)* B.Ed. | 190 | 17.868 | 3.884 | 24.768 | 5.898 | 13.432** |
| **II. Marital Status** | | | | | | |
| *(i)* Married | 200 | 18.606 | 4.028 | 26.998 | 6.264 | 16.138** |
| *(ii)* Unmarried | 160 | 17.625 | 2.691 | 21.943 | 3.586 | 12.337** |
| **III. Location** | | | | | | |
| *(i)* Rural | 180 | 18.028 | 3.622 | 23.444 | 5.226 | 11.398** |
| *(ii)* Urban | 180 | 19.517 | 3.588 | 26.039 | 6.371 | 11.934** |
| **IV. Type of Family** | | | | | | |
| **A. Married** | | | | | | |
| *(i)* Nuclear | 80 | 18.987 | 3.600 | 26.188 | 6.124 | 9.009** |
| *(ii)* Joint | 120 | 18.225 | 27.808 | 27.808 | 6.405 | 13.399** |

*(Contd.)*

*(Contd.)*

| *1* | *2* | *3* | *4* | *5* | *6* | *7* |
|---|---|---|---|---|---|---|
| **B. Unmarried** | | | | | | |
| *(i)* Nuclear | 80 | 17.950 | 2.846 | 21.600 | 3.101 | 7.708** |
| *(ii)* Joint | 80 | 17.300 | 2.537 | 22.287 | 4.072 | 9.240** |
| **V. Teaching Experience** | | | | | | |
| *(i)* More than five years | 220 | 18.436 | 4.052 | 26.627 | 6.316 | 16.152** |
| *(ii)* Less than five years | 140 | 17.664 | 2.701 | 21.893 | 3.664 | 10.953** |
| **VI. Financing and Management of School** | | | | | | |
| *(i)* Government | 80 | 17.950 | 2.846 | 21.600 | 3.101 | 7.708** |
| *(ii)* Aided | 130 | 18.077 | 3.749 | 23.392 | 5.100 | 9.538** |
| *(iii)* Private | 150 | 18.267 | 3.847 | 27.760 | 6.344 | 15.619** |
| **VII. Type of School** | | | | | | |
| *(i)* Girls School | 105 | 17.705 | 2.725 | 21.590 | 3.371 | 9.141** |
| *(ii)* Boys School | 120 | 17.800 | 4.053 | 24.258 | 5.165 | 10.731** |
| *(iii)* Co-educational | 135 | 18.748 | 3.717 | 27.815 | 6.577 | 13.892** |

**Significant at .01 level.

Conflict. It indicates that women teachers teaching in both rural and urban areas experience more intra job Role Conflict than inter job Role Conflict.

**IV. Type of Family**

Table 7.11 reveals that t-ratio being 9.009, 13.399 7.708 and 9.240 are significant at .01 level of significance. This shows that married and unmarried women teachers differ significantly on inter job Role Conflict than intra job Role Conflict. It also indicates that married and unmarried women teachers belonging to nuclear and joint families experience more intra job Role Conflict than inter job Role Conflict.

**V. Teaching Experience**

Table 7.11 reveals that t-ratio being 16.152 and 10.953 are significant at .01 level of significance. This shows that women teachers having teaching experience more than five years and less than five years differ significantly on inter job Role Conflict and intra job Role Conflict. It also indicates that women teachers having teaching experience of more than five years and less than five years are prone to more intra job Role Conflict than inter job Role Conflict.

**VI. Financing and Management of School**

Table 7.11 reveals that t-ratio being 7.708, 9.538 and 15.619 are significant at .01 level of significance. This shows that women teachers teaching in government schools, aided schools and private schools differ significantly on inter job Role Conflict and intra job Role Conflict. It also indicates that women teachers teaching in government schools, aided schools and private schools experience more intra job Role Conflict than inter job Role Conflict.

**VII. Type of School**

Table 7.11 reveals that t-ratio being 9.141, 10.731 and 13.892 are significant at .01 level of significance. It shows that women teachers teaching in girls schools, boys schools and co-educational schools differ significantly on inter job Role Conflict and intra job Role Conflict. It also indicates that women teachers teaching in girls schools, boys schools and co-educational schools experience more intra job Role Conflict than inter job Role Conflict.

# 8 Main Findings, Discussion of Results, Educational Implications and Suggestions for Further Research

On the basis of analysis and interpretation of data as presented in the foregoing chapters, the following main findings and discussion of the results are given below :

## 8.1 MAIN FINDINGS

The major aspects upon which the main findings depend are :

8.1.1 The distribution of Role Conflict Scores among women teachers.

8.1.2 Incidence of Role Conflict among women teachers.

8.1.3 Correlation between Role Conflict and Personality Factors among women teachers.

8.1.4 Correlation between Role Conflict and Personality Factors with respect to demographic variables.

8.1.5 Correlation between Role Conflict and Socio-economic Status of women teachers.

8.1.6 Comparison of Role Conflict among women teachers with respect to demographic variables.

8.1.7 Comparison of *(a)* inter-family Role Conflict, *(b)* intra-family Role Conflict among women teachers with respect to demographic variables.

8.1.8 Comparison of *(a)* inter-job Role Conflict and *(b)* intra-job Role Conflict, among women teachers with respect to demographic variables.

8.1.9 Comparison of inter-family Role Conflict and intra-family Role Conflict among women teachers with respect to demographic variables.

8.1.10 Comparison of inter-job Role Conflict and intra-job Role Conflict among women teachers with respect to demographic variables.

### 8.1.1 The Distribution of Role Conflict Scores among Women Teachers

The distribution of Role Conflict scores among women teachers is normal.

### 8.1.2 Incidence of Role Conflict among Women Teachers

Incidence of Role Conflict among women teachers is calculated through percentiles. Mean scores of Role Conflict are also derived and represented through histograms. It reveals that married women teachers experience the highest Role Conflict and unmarried women teachers experience the lowest Role Conflict. Teaching experience also affects a lot the Role Conflict faced by women teachers. It also suggests that women teachers belonging to nuclear family experience more Role Conflict in comparison to women teachers belonging to joint family. The study also reveals that women teachers working in urban schools are prone to high Role Conflict than their rural counterparts. The study shows that women teachers working in aided and private schools experience more Role Conflict than their counterparts working in government schools. The educational qualification does not make much difference in the level of Role Conflict experienced by J.B.T. as well as B.Ed. women teachers.

### 8.1.3 Correlation between Role Conflict and Personality Factors among Women Teachers

*(a)* Product moment coefficients of correlation between Role Conflict and Personality Factors G, H, L, $Q_2$ and $Q_3$ are found to be positive and significant among women teachers. This shows that Personality Factors conscientious, venturesome, suspicious, self sufficient and controlled lead to increase the total Role Conflict. There exists negative and significant correlations

between Role Conflict and Personality Factors E and $Q_4$ which show that humble and relaxed women teachers experience high Role Conflict.

*(b)* There are significant and positive correlations between inter Role Conflict and Personality Factors C, G, H, L, $Q_2$ and $Q_3$. This shows that emotionally less stable, conscientious, venturesome, suspicious, self sufficient and controlled Personality Factors lead to increase inter Role Conflict. There is a negative and significant correlation between inter Role Conflict and Personality Factor $Q_4$. This reveals that relaxed women teachers experience high inter Role Conflict.

*(c)* There are positive and significant correlations between intra Role Conflict and Personality Factors G, L, O, and $Q_2$ which shows that Personality Factors conscientious, suspicious, troubled, and self sufficient lead to increase Intra-Role Conflict. There are negative and significant correlations between intra Role Conflict and Personality Factors A, E and $Q_4$ which reveal that Personality Factors reserved, humble and relaxed women teachers experience high Intra Role Conflict.

*(d)* There are positive and significant correlations between family Role Conflict and Personality Factors C, H, M, G, L, $Q_2$ and $Q_3$. This shows that emotionally less stable, venturesome, imaginative, conscientious, suspicious, self sufficient and controlled Personality Factors lead to high Role Conflict. There exists negative and significant correlations between family Role Conflict and Personality Factors E, and $Q_4$. This reveals that humble and relaxed women teachers experience high family Role Conflict.

*(e)* There are positive and significant correlations between job Role Conflict and Personality Factors G, H, L, $Q_2$ and $Q_3$. This shows that conscientious, venturesome, suspicious, self sufficient and controlled women teachers experience high job Role Conflict. There are negative and significant correlations between job Role

Conflict and Personality Factors E and $Q_4$. This shows that humble and relaxed women teachers experience high job Role Conflict.

### 8.1.4 Correlations between Role Conflict and Personality Factors with respect to Demographic Variables

*(a)* There are positive and significant correlations between Role Conflict and Personality Factors G, and $Q_3$. This shows that Personality Factors conscientious and controlled lead to increase Role Conflict. There are also negative and significant correlations between Role Conflict and Personality Factors E and $Q_4$ which shows that humble and relaxed J.B.T. women teachers experience high Role Conflict.

*(b)* There are positive and significant correlations between Role Conflict and Personality Factors G, H, L, $Q_2$ and $Q_3$. This shows that conscientious, venturesome, suspicious, self sufficient and controlled women teachers experience high Role Conflict. There is also a negative correlation between Role Conflict and Personality Factor B which is significant. This reveals that less intelligent B.Ed. women teachers experience high Role Conflict.

*(c)* There is a negative and significant correlation between Role Conflict and Personality Factor 'I' of married women teachers. This shows that tough minded married women teachers experience high Role Conflict.

*(d)* There is a negative and significant correlation between Role Conflict and Personality Factor 'A'. This shows that reserved unmarried women teachers experience high Role Conflict.

*(e)* There are positive and significant correlations between Role Conflict and Personality factors G, N, M and O. This shows that conscientious, shrewd, imaginative and apprehensive women teachers working in rural areas experience high Role Conflict. There is also a negative and significant correlation between Role

Conflict and Personality Factors F and $Q_4$. This shows that sober and relaxed women teachers working in rural areas experience high Role Conflict.

*(f)* There are positive and significant correlations between Role Conflict and Personality Factors L and M. This shows that experience and imaginative women-teachers experience high Role Conflict. There is also negative and significant correlation between Role Conflict and Personality Factor B. This shows that less intelligent women teachers working in urban schools experience high Role Conflict.

*(g)* There is a negative and significant correlation between Role Conflict and Personality Factor B. This shows that less intelligent women teachers belonging to nuclear family experience high Role Conflict.

*(h)* There are positive and significant correlations between Role Conflict and Personality Factors B, G, M and N. This reveals that bright, conscientious, imaginative and shrewd women teachers experience high Role Conflict. There are also negative and significant correlations between Role Conflict and Personality Factors F and $Q_4$. This suggests that sober and relaxed women teachers belonging to joint family experience high Role Conflict.

*(i)* There are positive and significant correlations between Role Conflict and Personality Factors E, F and I. This shows that assertive, happy-go-lucky, and tender-minded women teachers experience high Role Conflict. There are negative and significant correlations between Role Conflict and Personality Factors N and $Q_4$. This shows that forthright and relaxed women teachers with more than 5 years of teaching experience are prone to high Role Conflict.

*(j)* There are positive and significant correlations between Role Conflict and Personality Factors A, E, F, G, M, $Q_2$ and $Q_4$ among teachers with less than 5 years of teaching experience. This reveals that outgoing,

assertive, happy-go-lucky, conscientious, imaginative, self-sufficient, and tense women teachers experience high Role Conflict.

*(k)* There are positive and significant correlations between Role Conflict and Personality Factors F, G, H, N, $Q_1$ and I. This shows that happy-go-lucky, conscientious, venturesome, shrewd, liberal and tender-minded women teachers working in government schools experience high Role Conflict. There is a negative and significant correlation between Role Conflict and Personality Factor L which shows that trusting women teachers experience high Role Conflict.

*(l)* There are positive and significant correlations between Role Conflict and Personality Factors I, L, M, N, $Q_4$, O and $O_3$. This shows that tender-minded, suspicious, imaginative, shrewd, tense, apprehensive and controlled women teachers working in aided schools experience high Role Conflict. There are also negative and significant correlations between Role Conflict and Personality Factors A, G and $Q_1$. This reveals that reserved, expedient and conservative women teachers working in aided schools experience high Role Conflict.

*(m)* There are positive and significant correlations between Role Conflict and Personality Factors F, G, H, $Q_1$, $Q_2$ and $Q_4$. This suggests that happy-go-lucky, conscientious, venturesome, liberal, self-sufficient and tense women teachers working in private schools experience high Role Conflict.

*(n)* There are positive and significant correlations between Role Conflict and Personality Factors A, E, H, M, O, $Q_1$ and $Q_4$. This shows that outgoing, assertive, venturesome, imaginative, liberal and tense women teachers working in girls schools experience high Role Conflict. There are negative and significant correlations between Role Conflict and Personality Factors I and L. This suggests that tough minded and trusting women teachers working in girls schools experience high Role Conflict.

(o) There are positive and significant correlations between Role Conflict and Personality Factors A, E, G, I, M, $Q_2$ and $Q_4$. This reveals that outgoing, assertive, conscientious, tenderminded, imaginative, self-sufficient and tense women teachers working in boys schools experience high Role Conflict. There is a negative and significant correlation between Role Conflict and Personality Factor L. This shows that trusting women teachers working in boys schools experience high Role Conflict.

(p) There are positive and significant correlations between Role Conflict and Personality Factors A, G, I, N and $Q_1$. It shows that outgoing, conscientious, tender-minded, shrewd and liberal women teachers working in co-educational schools experience high Role Conflict. There is also a negative and significant correlation between Role Conflict and Personality Factor $Q_4$ which shows that relaxed women teachers experience high Role Conflict.

### 8.1.5 Coefficients of Correlation between Role Conflict and Socio-economic Status of Women Teachers

There is negative and significant correlation between total Role Conflict and Socio-economic Status of upper lower class women teachers. This shows that lower the Socio-economic Status, higher will be the Role Conflict among women teachers of upper lower class. It also indicates that there exists insignificant correlations between Role Conflict and other categories of Socio-economic Status *i.e.* middle class and upper middle class of women teachers. It suggests that there exists no relationship between Role Conflict and Socio-economic Status of women teachers belonging to upper middle and middle class.

### 8.1.6 Comparison of Role Conflict among Women Teachers with respect to Demographic Variables

(a) J.B.T. and B.Ed. women teachers are significantly different on intra Role Conflict. This shows that J.B.T. women teachers experience more intra Role Conflict than B.Ed women teachers.

(b) Married and unmarried women teachers differ significantly on Role Conflict. It also indicates that married women teachers experience more Role Conflict except intra Role Conflict than unmarried women teachers.

(c) Women teachers working in rural and urban areas differ significantly on Role Conflict. It shows that women teachers working in urban areas experience more Role Conflict than women teachers working in rural areas.

(d) Women teachers differ significantly with respect to their type of family they belong. This shows that women teachers belonging to nuclear families experience more Role Conflict than women teachers belonging to joint families except on Intra Role Conflict whereas women teachers belonging to joint families experience more Intra Role Conflict than women teachers belonging to nuclear families.

(e) Women teachers having less than five years of teaching experience and more than five years of teaching experience differ significantly on Role Conflict. This shows that women teachers having less than five years of teaching experience face more Role Conflict than their counterparts having more than five years of teaching experience.

(f) Women teachers working in government schools, aided schools and private schools are significantly different on Role Conflict. This shows that women teachers working in aided and private schools experience more Role Conflict than their counterparts working in government schools. It also suggests that women teachers working in aided schools experience more Intra Role Conflict than their counterparts working in private schools.

(g) Women teachers working in girls schools, boys schools and co-educational schools are significantly different on Role Conflict. This shows that women teachers working in boys schools experience more inter Role Conflict and family Role Conflict than their counterparts working on girls schools. This also suggests that women teachers working in co-educational schools experience more Role Conflict than those working in girls schools except on intra Role Conflict and family Role Conflict. It also reveals that women teachers working in co-educational schools experience more social Role Conflict than those working in boys schools.

### 8.1.7 Comparison of *(a)* Inter-Family Role Conflict and *(b)* Intra Family Role Conflict among Women Teachers with respect to Demographic Variables

*(a)* J.B.T. and B.Ed women teachers differ significantly on intra family Role Conflict. It shows that B.Ed. women teachers experience more intra family Role Family than that of J.B.T. women teachers.

*(b)* Married and unmarried women teachers are significantly different on inter family Role Conflict. This shows that married women teachers experience more inter family Role Conflict than unmarried women teachers.

*(c)* Women teachers working in rural and urban areas are significantly different on inter family Role Conflict. It suggests that women teachers working in urban areas experience more inter family Role Conflict than their counterparts working in rural areas.

*(d)* Married and unmarried women teachers are also significantly different on inter-family Role Conflict and intra family Role Conflict belonging to nuclear and joint families. This shows that married women teachers experience more inter family Role Conflict than unmarried women teachers living in nuclear families and unmarried women teachers experience more intra family Role Conflict than married women teachers belonging to nuclear families. It also suggests that married women teachers experience more inter family

Role Conflict than their unmarried counterparts living in joint families.

(e) Women teachers having more than five years of teaching experience and less than five years of teaching experience are significantly different on inter family Role Conflict. This shows that women teachers having more than five years of teaching experience are prone to more inter family Role Conflict than those of having less than five years of teaching experience.

(f) Women teachers working in government schools, aided schools and private schools differ significantly on inter family Role Conflict and intra family Role Conflict. It shows that women teachers working in aided and private schools experience more inter family Role Conflict than their counterparts working in government schools. It also suggests that women teachers working in private schools experience more inter family Role Conflict than those working in aided schools whereas women teachers working in aided schools experience more intra family Role Conflict than those working in private schools.

(g) Women teachers working in girls schools, boys schools and co-educational schools are significantly differ on inter-family Role Conflict and intra family Role Conflict. This shows that women teachers working in boys schools experience more inter-family Role Conflict than those working in girls schools. This also suggests that women teachers working in co-educational schools experience more inter family Role Conflict than those working in girls schools and boys schools. The women teachers working in girls schools and boys schools experience more intra family Role Conflict than their counterparts working in co-educational schools.

### 8.1.8 Comparison of *(a)* Inter-Job Role Conflict and *(b)* Intra-Job Role Conflict Among Women Teachers with Respect to Demographic Variables

(a) Married and unmarried women teachers differ

significantly on intra job Role Conflict. It suggests that married women teachers experience more intra job conflict than their unmarried counterparts.

*(b)* Women teachers working in rural and urban areas differ significantly on inter job and intra job Role Conflict. It shows that women teachers working in urban areas experience more inter job Role Conflict and intra job Role Conflict than those working in rural areas.

*(c)* Married and unmarried women teachers living in nuclear families or joint families are significantly different on inter job Role Conflict and intra job Role Conflict. It shows that married women teachers experience more inter job Role Conflict as well as intra job Role Conflict living in nuclear and joint families.

*(d)* Women teachers with more than five years of teaching experience and less than five years of teaching experience differ significantly on inter job Role Conflict and intra job Role Conflict. It suggests that women teachers having more than five years of teaching experience are prone to more inter job Role Conflict and intra job Role Conflict than those of having less than five years of teaching experience.

*(e)* Women teachers working in government schools, aided schools and private schools differ significantly on intra job Role Conflict. It suggests that women teachers working in private schools experience more intra job Role Conflict than those working in government and aided schools.

*(f)* Women teachers working in girls schools, boys schools and co-educational schools differ significantly on intra job conflict. It shows that women teachers working in boys schools and co-educational schools experience more intra job Role Conflict than those working in girls schools. It also shows that women teachers working in co-educational schools experience more intra job Role Conflict than those working in girls schools and boys schools.

### 8.1.9 Comparison of Inter Family Role Conflict and Intra Family Role Conflict with Respect to Demographic Variables

*(a)* J.B.T. women teachers differ significantly on inter family Role Conflict and intra family Role Conflict. It shows that J.B.T. women teachers experience more inter family Role Conflict than intra family Role Conflict.

*(b)* Married and unmarried women teachers differ significantly on inter family Role Conflict and intra family Role Conflict. Married women teachers experience more inter family Role Conflict whereas unmarried women teachers experience more intra family Role Conflict.

*(c)* Women teachers working in urban areas differ significantly on inter family Role Conflict and intra family Role Conflict. It shows that women teachers working in urban areas experience more inter family Role Conflict than intra family Role Conflict.

*(d)* Married and unmarried women teachers belonging to nuclear and joint family are significantly different on inter family Role Conflict and intra family Role Conflict. It shows that married women teachers belonging to nuclear and joint families experience more intra family Role Conflict than unmarried women teachers belonging to nuclear and joint families.

*(e)* Women teachers having more than five years of teaching experience and less than five years of teaching experience are significantly different on inter family Role Conflict and intra family Role Conflict. It shows that women teachers having more than five years of teaching experience are prone to more inter family Role Conflict than intra family Role Conflict, whereas women teachers having less than five years of teaching experience are prone to more intra family Role Conflict than inter family Role Conflict.

*(f)* Women teachers working in government schools,

aided schools and private schools are significantly different on inter family Role Conflict and intra family Role Conflict. It shows that women teachers working in government schools and aided schools experience more intra family Role Conflict than inter family Role Conflict whereas women teachers working in private schools are prone to high inter family Role Conflict than intra family Role Conflict.

*(g)* Women teachers working in girls schools and boys schools are significantly different on inter family Role Conflict and intra family Role Conflict. It shows that women teachers working in girls schools experience more intra family Role Conflict than inter family Role Conflict, whereas women teachers working in co-educational schools experience more inter family Role Conflict than intra family Role Conflict.

### 8.1.10 Comparison of Inter Job Conflict and Intra Job Role Conflict Among Women Teachers with Respect to Demographic Variables

Women teachers with respect to various demographic variables such as J.B.T./B.Ed, married/unmarried, rural/urban, nuclear family/joint family, more than five years/less than five years of teaching experience, government schools/aided schools/private schools and girls schools/boys schools/co-educational schools are significantly different on inter job Role Conflict and intra job Role Conflict. This suggests that all women teachers experience more intra job Role Conflict than inter job Role Conflict.

## 8.2 DISCUSSION OF RESULTS

The present study was conducted with respect to Role Conflict among women teachers. From the frequency polygon, it was found that the distribution of Role Conflict scores among women teachers is normal.

Women teachers experience Role Conflict but it varies with respect to aforesaid demographic variables.

From the coefficients of correlation between Role Conflict

and Personality Factors, it is found that conscientious (G) suspicious (L), self-sufficient ($Q_2$) and relaxed ($Q_4$) Personality Factors lead to increase the Role Conflict including total Role Conflict, inter Role Conflict, intra Role Conflict, family Role Conflict, job Role Conflict, social Role Conflict, and dual Role Conflict *i.e.* home role as well as job Role Conflict. This shows that women teachers with stronger super-ego strength, suspicious, self-sufficient, and relaxed PF experience more Role Conflict. Indirectly, the results of the study was supported by the study of Fontana and Abuouserie (1993) that there exists relationship between Role Conflict and Personality traits.

The results of the study also reveal that Personality Factor (E) *i.e.* humble, submissive women teachers experience high Role Conflict excluding inter Role Conflict. It may be possible that humble women teachers being dependent and passive, may postpone certain duties for the next day or the other And at times, they may get confused to do or not to do, which ultimately leads to Role Conflict. Venturesome and uninhibited (H) women teachers experience high Role Conflict except intra Role Conflict. This may be possible that these women teachers are socially bold and try to do new things and are also abundant in emotional response due to which, they experience overall more Role Conflict.

The study also reveals that women teachers who are also socially precise ($Q_3$) *i.e.* controlled, experience high Role Conflict except intra Role Conflict. This may be explained on the basis that these women teachers being socially aware, careful, also try to obey and regard social norms. By doing so, a working woman feels herself torn between personal interests and social interests which lead to high Role Conflict.

It is also found that women teachers with higher ego strength (C) experience more inter Role Conflict and family Role Conflict. It may be possible that some times such women teachers try to maintain solid group morale and try to make a resigned adjustment to unsolved emotional problems. Meanwhile, the situation becomes incompatible to meet and she gets entangled in inter Role Conflict and family Role Conflict.

The study shows that Personality Factor contributing to Role Conflict is resourcefulness ($Q_2$) of a person. Such self-sufficient women teachers try to do the things on their own way which may prove contradictory and simultaneous in its nature. Therefore, this leads to Role Conflict *i.e.* total Role Conflict, inter Role Conflict, intra Role Conflict, family Role Conflict, job Role Conflict, social Role Conflict and dual Role Conflict *i.e.* home role as well as job Role Conflict. The results show that Personality Factor *i.e.* relaxed ($Q_4$) is associated to Role Conflict. It may be due to that sometimes over satisfaction can lead to laziness and low performance which cause conflict among her respective roles. The results of the study also suggested that Personality Factor *i.e.* suspicious (L) is very much related to Role Conflict. The reason for this may be the fact that suspicious women teachers are usually deliberate in their actions and self opinionated which directly lead to confusion in one's mind and thereby cause role ambiguity.

It was also found that Personality Factor (G) *i.e.* conscientious, and rule-bound women teachers are prone to high Role Conflict. It may be possible that such women are dominated by the sense of duty. Therefore, assuming the responsibility to do everything by herself can lead to high Role Conflict including total Role Conflict, inter Role Conflict, intra Role Conflict, family Role Conflict, job Role Conflict, social Role Conflict and dual Role Conflict.

Personality Factor (A) *i.e.* reserved women teachers experience more Role Conflict. It may be possible that reserved persons may tend at times to be critical and obstructive. They are liable to do things in their own way which is directly related to intra Role Conflict. The study also reveal that Personality Factor (M) *i.e.* imaginative women teachers experience high family Role Conflict. There is difference between realm of imagination and reality. When a women does not find her imagination translated into real life situations then it leads to family Role Conflict.

The study also reveals that Personality Factor of low intelligence (B) leads to Role Conflict among B.Ed women teachers and urban women teachers. The reason for this may be that less intelligent persons tend to represent poor functioning in respective tasks or roles which leads to slacking of duties and obligations on her part which increases to Role Conflict.

The study reveals that Personality Factor (I) *i.e.* tough mindedness leads to more Role Conflict in married women teachers. Possibly that such women being independent, responsible may try to fulfil the needs and demands of their near and dear. As it becomes difficulty for a working women to come up to their expectations in certain circumstances and that is why she experiences Role Conflict on her own way.

It was also found that unmarried women teachers are reserved (A) in their nature and experience more Role Conflict. The reason for this may be that being working alone and doing things in their own way at times may tend to be critical and hard which leads to Role Conflict.

The Personality Factor sober (F) leads to high Role Conflict among rural women teachers. It may be due to the reason that being passimistic and dependable, sometimes, may prove false which creates stress in their minds and Role Conflict is observed by them. It was also suggested that Personality Factor (N) *i.e.* shrewd rural women teachers experience high Role Conflict. This may be possible that being hard headed and having an unsentimental approach to situations may lead to high Role Conflict.

The Personality Factor, low intelligence (B) leads to high Role Conflict among nuclear families. It may be due to the fact that poor functioning on the part of women in her nuclear family seems impracticable. So, due to failure of duties, a woman teacher experiences high Role Conflict. The study reveals that Personality Factor forthright (N) leads to high Role Conflict. It may be possible that such artless women teachers cannot keep pace with the increasing demands of their joint families and it leads to high Role Conflict.

It was also found that Personality Factor free thinking ($Q_1$) leads to high Role Conflict among women teachers working in government schools, urban schools, private schools, girls schools, and co-educational schools. This may be due to the fact that such women teachers have doubts on fundamental issues and are inclined to experiment in life generally, hence Role Conflict is unavoidable during such situations at present times.

The coefficients of correlation between Role Conflict and Socio-economic Status of women teachers is negative and significant which shows that low Socio-Economic Status leads to increase Role Conflict among women teachers belonging to upper lower class. It may be due to the reason that limited resources do not allow them to take the advantage of servant in the family. The other factors such as large family, poor health and working conditions, low salary non-cooperative attitude of the Head which leads to Role Conflict among women teachers.

It was found that J.B.T. and B.Ed women teachers are significantly different on intra Role Conflict. The study reveals that J.B.T. women teachers experience more intra Role Conflict that B.Ed women teachers. It may be possible that J.B.T. women teachers have to perform more mental work as they have to mould the raw material (younger generations) in the schools from very beginning in comparison to B.Ed women teachers. The second factor may be lack of maturity on the part of J.B.T. women teachers. The studies of Hatta and Nishiide (1991) supported some of the findings that primary school teachers experience greater subjective stress mood. However, no study was found to be conducted on women teachers. On the other, intra family Role Conflict is found in B.Ed. women teachers whereas J.B.T. women teachers experience more inter family Role Conflict.

The study reveals that married women teachers experience more Role Conflict except intra Role Conflict than unmarried women teachers. This may be due to multiple roles and different socio-economic backgrounds after marriage in case of married women teachers. Unmarried women teachers experience more intra-family Role Conflict than married one.

This may be due to lack of sharing conflicts or things with some one close to unmarried women teachers. The other reason may be specific social constraints and social norms in case of unmarried women. Whereas married women teachers experience more inter-family Role Conflict than their unmarried counterparts. The reason for this may be the role priorities confusion in case of married women teachers. The studies of Yogev and Brett (1985), Greenhaus and Parasuraman (1986), Miles (1977), Nevil and Demico (1975), Johnson and Johson (1976), Shaw and Costanzo (1970), Rani (1976), Abdel-Halim (1978) support the similar findings.

It is also found that women teachers working in urban areas experience more Role Conflict than their counterparts working in rural areas. The possible reason for this is that the rural women have less material demands on their family members and lack of awareness is much common on the part of rural women also. Indirectly, the results are supported by the studies of Seidman (1989), Carpenter (1989) who state that location is a critical barrier to personal and professional development in case of women teachers.

The results also reveal that women teachers belonging to nuclear families experience more Role Conflict than those belonging to joint family except on intra Role Conflict. It may be possible reason that child-care problem for married women teachers is much prevalent in nuclear family and there may be more family work demands on a woman in nuclear family also. But intra Role Conflict among women teachers in their joint families is due to the presence of varied interests of varied persons present in such families which create a number of problems within a single role in family. Unmarried women teachers also experience more intra family Role Conflict which may be due to restricted social mobility and familial constraints on female working behaviour.

The results also indicate that women teachers having less than five years of teaching experience face more Role Conflict than those having more than five years of teaching experience. It is clear that with the passage of time, efficiency of teachers get increased, hence so many problems get solved automatically with the experience at home as well as at work place *i.e.* school. The another possible reason is that bookish knowledge among new comer teacher and new school environment cannot meet the practical situation. Indirectly, the results of the present study can be supported in the light of the results of study of Rice (1990) who state that new school environment affects the new comer teachers' efficiency.

On the other hand, the results show that women teachers having more than five years of teaching experience are prone to more inter job and inter family Role Conflict than those of having less than five years of teaching experience. This may be due to the fact that responsibilities and demands of elder children go on increasing with the time. And personal interest clash with professional interest. This finding is supported by the results of the study by Grace (1974) who state that teachers with more than 10 years of teaching experience perceived significantly more conflict than those of less experienced teachers.

The study also unfolds that women teachers having less than five years of teaching experience are prone to intra family Role Conflict. This may be the cause of lack of maturity of understanding, indecisive attitude towards a role, may contribute to intra family Role Conflict among women teachers having less than five years of teaching experience.

The results of significant differences with respect to financing and management of schools show that women teachers working aided and private schools experience more Role Conflict including inter family Role Conflict than those working in government schools. The possible reason is that women teachers working in aided and private schools are meagrely paid but have to meet more work demands. Job dissatisfaction, exploitation by Heads and lack of job securities may also contribute to Role Conflict among women teachers working in aided and private schools. Women teachers working in aided schools experience more intra Role Conflict than those working in private schools.

The finding of the study also reported that women teachers working in boys schools, and co-educational schools experience more Role Conflict than those working in girls schools. It may be due to the social as well as familial constraints on women teachers to work only in girls schools. It also reveals that women teachers working in co-educational schools experience more social Role Conflict than those working in boys schools. This may be possible due to the fact that a woman teacher may be criticised by neighbourers, parents—in-laws or husbands, if she invites or mixes with male colleagues and or male students. She also takes both boys and girls into full consideration during teaching learning process for instance during biology classes.

## 8.3 EDUCATIONAL IMPLICATIONS

The results derived from the findings of this research study, the following educational implications are drawn :

Since the scale for the assessment of Role Conflict among women teachers has been constructed and standardized by the investigator as a part of this research work, it is quite worth to make frequent use of it in various studies. Role Conflict Scale (RCS) can serve as a potential measure in the field of conflict management.

One of the results has made a revelation that married women teachers experience more Role Conflict as compared to their unmarried counterparts. Some of the personality traits for married women teachers for both inter and intra Role Conflict were found to be emotionally less stable, suspicious, relaxed, conscientious, venturesome etc. Married women teachers should remain vigilant regarding this fact that they should avoid as far as possible the Role Conflict encountered by them at home as well as school situations.

The results of this study signify that women teachers working in urban areas face more Role Conflict as compared to their colleagues working in rural areas. May be that the schools situated in rural configuration present more easy and cooperative environment as compared to those of urban areas.

Such type of conditions of ease and cooperation should also be developed in the urban schools so as to enable the women teachers to reduce their role conflict.

The women teachers living in nuclear families face more Role Conflict as compared to those who are living in joint family system. This indicates that joint family system has much to contribute towards releasing the Role Conflict among women teachers. Moreover, when women teachers are not at their respective homes, their children are well looked after in joint family system. The results suggest that joint family system should be encouraged as far possible.

Women working in aided schools are found to face more Role Conflict than those who are working in government and private schools. Lesser salaries and that too are not timely paid has become permanent features of aided schools. The salaries to the teachers of such schools should be given through treasuries and government should keep a close watch that teachers in general and women teachers in particular are getting it regularly. Besides this, such institutions should be encouraged to strengthen their financial conditions by raising funds through organising other social activities.

The results of the present work has shown that women teachers working in co-educational schools face more Role Conflict as compared to their counterparts working in girls and boys schools. This is because of the fact that boys as well as girls schools provide more ease whereas co-educational schools present a chaotic look. Co-educational schools face multiple problems which should as far as possible appointed in girls schools where as male teachers should work in boys schools. When it comes to co-educational schools, provision of separate sections of girls should be made. It will enable women teachers to reduce their Role Conflict to some extent.

## SUGGESTIONS FOR FURTHER STUDY

1. The study can be conducted on a larger sample from both rural and urban areas.
2. Effect of other variables like number of children,

number of dependents, teacher-competency, age, self concept, job satisfaction and life satisfaction in relation to Role Conflict can be explored among working women including women teachers also.

3. Comparative studies on Role Conflict can be conducted with reference to different levels of teaching *i.e.* primary, secondary, senior secondary and higher also among male as well as female teachers.
4. Comparative studies on correlates of Role Conflict among working and non-working women can be conducted.
5. Such studies can be conducted on different disciplines of teaching *i.e.* Arts and Science teachers.
6. A study of Role Conflict can also be undertaken with a view to compare the life satisfaction of skilled, semi-skilled, and unskilled categories of working women.
7. Role Conflict can also be studied in relation to Role Conflict resolution system.
8. Similar studies can also be conducted on non-working educated women, uneducated women, students, teachers, heads of various institutions and male population of the state.
9. It may be suggested that there is a need of deeper probing into the problem. An interview of the family members, parents-in-laws, neighbourers, employer of working women including women teachers will be very useful.

# Summary

May it be home or office, factory or farm, sowing field or scavenger site—a woman's role has always been prominent especially from the work point of view in almost all the times.

The deplorable condition of women remained unchanged throughout the Hindu and Muslim periods. But after sometimes, the spread of English education and intermingling of western and eastern cultures enabled the Indian woman to realize and regain her legitimate status.

The advent of the Second World War resulted into some important changes in Socio-economic Status of women and their social relationships. The United Nations Organisations reaffirmed faith in the fundamental human rights, in the dignity and worth of the human beings and also in the equal rights of men and women.

Post Independence period brought much success to women who till now were striving hard to get their due. Many drastic changes in women's work and family roles brought about tangible implications for employment and family policy.

Both in cities and villages, women are taking more and more jobs by breaking the social-psychological barrier. They are employed as teachers, doctors, lawyers, nurses, engineers, journalists, officers in the government departments as well as in non-government sectors.

The role of woman as a school teacher is important as she makes noteworthy contribution in the holy task of building the future of the country.

As woman teachers perform more than one role simultaneously, so multiplicity of roles is inevitable among them which creates confusion regarding their roles. The cycle of Role Conflict goes on between expectations of others and expectations by oneself. Sometimes there is a problem between two roles which take place at one time and for another time there is conflict due to the expectations attached to a single role.

## CONCEPT OF ROLE CONFLICT

Role Conflict takes place in certain situations *i.e.* the role player is required to perform simultaneously two or more roles that present contradictory expectations. And it is not possible for an actor to conform to those conflicting expectations. That is what usually happens when a women has to perform simultaneously roles of a housewife and a teacher. In this context, Linton (1945) and Goffman (1961) state that because of different personality characteristics and dispositions, the Role Conflict may become noticeable.

Role Conflict may be categorised in the following way :

**(a) Inter Role Conflict**

It occurs when a person occupies two positions simultaneously (Sarbin, 1954).

**(b) Intra Role Conflict**

It occurs from a number of sources within a specific role (Nye, 1980).

In addition to her usual jobs a woman teacher has to discharge a number of duties and responsibilities related to her specific roles. The performance of simultaneous and incompatible duties give rise to Role Conflict. The conflict may arise due to normative and conflicting expectations. It is generally felt that a married woman teacher experience greater conflict than unmarried and non-working women to her family roles and job roles. It may be because of the simultaneous and incompatible nature of roles.

Personality of a women teacher also affects Role Conflict. By personality, it is meant that the individual's physical and mental patterns with the help of which he/she acts. Personality is the total quality of an individual due to which bodily pattern, mental integration and chemistry of internal organs' functions.

There are various demographic variables namely educational level, marital status, location of school, type of family, teaching experience, financing and management of school and type of school which may also affect the Role Conflict of women teachers working in various schools.

## JUSTIFICATION OF THE STUDY

Being a teacher, women can not carry out efficiently each of her roles as a wife, mother, teacher, housewife and social being. Many times, she suffers from guilty conscience and finds herself torn between home, school and society. Due to the non-cooperative attitude of her husband and other family members she becomes more tense. Her family and social life suffers in marital disharmony and marital frictions. This condition creates social and psychological problems.

A teacher can teach well if she is happy and satisfied. The adjustment or maladjustment of a teacher significantly affects her home role, job role and social role which in the long run lays an indelible impact on the nation in general and the group in particular to which she belongs.

It was proposed to study the Role Conflict of women teachers of Haryana in relation to socio-psychological correlates with respect to some demographic variables.

## TITLE OF THE THESIS

"A study of socio-psychological correlates of conflict between family role and job role among women teachers".

## OBJECTIVES OF THE STUDY

1. To construct and standardize a Role Conflict Scale (RCS) for women teachers.
2. To study the nature and incidence of Role Conflict among women teachers.
3. To study the socio-psychological correlates of Role Conflict among women teachers with respect to Personality Factors, Socio-economic Status, educational level, marital status, type of school, location of school,

financing and management of school, type of family and teaching experience.

4. To find out the differences of Role Conflict experienced by women teachers with respect to their educational level, marital status, type of school, location of school, financing and management of school, type of family and teaching experience.

## HYPOTHESES

The following null hypotheses were framed to realise the aforesaid objectives of the study.

1. The Role Conflict among women teachers is not normally distributed.
2. There do not exist significant relationships between Role Conflict and various Socio-psychological correlates (such as Personality Factors and Socio-economic Status with respect to educational level, marital status, type of school, location of school, financing and management of school, type of family and teaching experience).
3. There do not exist significant differences in the mean scores of Role Conflict experienced by women teachers with respect to their educational level, marital status, type of school, location of school, financing and management of school, type of family and teaching experience.

## DELIMITATIONS OF THE STUDY

1. The study is delimited to 360 women teachers randomly drawn out from the state of Haryana.
2. The study is delimited to study the Role Conflict experienced by women teachers included in the present work.
3. The study is confined to two socio-psychological correlates *i.e.* Personality Factors and Socio-economic Status.

4. The study is conducted under the light of following variables, *i.e.,* educational level, marital status, type of school, location of school, financing and management of school, type of family and teaching experience.
5. Only inter-role conflict, intra role conflict, family role conflict, job role conflict, social role conflict and dual role conflict come under the purview of this study.

## RESEARCH METHODOLOGY

The present methodology of this study is based on descriptive research. Descriptive research not only concerns itself with formulation and testing of hypothesis but also analysing the relationship existing between various variables. The stress is also laid on the generalization developed from the piece of research. Thus, the descriptive method was considered most appropriate for conducting the study of women teachers. In this study, Role Conflict of women teachers was taken as dependent variable and Personality Factors, and some demographic variables including Socio-economic Status were taken as independent variables.

### Population and Sample

The women teachers working in the various schools in the state of Haryana constituted population for the present study. But it was difficult to include all of them in the purview of this work keeping in mind time, physical and financial constraints. That in why it was decided to select a small proportion of them for the sake of conducting this research study.

### Size and Sample

The investigator procured a list of all the primary and secondary schools from the offices of the District Education Officers and randomly selected a total number of 75 schools from 6 districts *i.e.* Hisar, Kurukshetra, Karnal, Kaithal, Yamuna Nagar and Ambala. While selecting these schools, only government, private and aided schools were considered. Thus, as many as 360 women teachers (an equal number of women teachers working in rural and urban areas *i.e.* 180 each) randomly picked up from boys, girls and co-educational schools constituted the sample.

**Tools Used**

*(a)* Role Conflict Scale for women teachers prepared by the investigator herself.

*(b)* Socio-economic Status Scale by R. Bhardwaj, S. Gupta and N.S. Chauhan.

*(c)* 16 Personality Factors Questionnaire (Form A) by R.B. Cattell and H.W. Eber.

**Classification of the Data**

The data thus collected for testing the hypotheses were classified on the basis of the following demographic variables :

*(a)* Educational level in terms of J.B.T. and B.Ed.

*(b)* Marital Status in terms of married and unmarried.

*(c)* Location of the school, *i.e.* rural and urban.

*(d)* Type of family *i.e.* nuclear and joint.

*(e)* Teaching experience *i.e.* more than 5 years and less than 5 years.

*(f)* Financing and Management of the school *i.e.* government aided and private.

*(g)* Type of school, *i.e.* girls, boys and co-educational.

## STATISTICAL TECHNIQUES USED

The following techniques were used for analysis of the data :

1. K-S Test was employed to study the nature of distribution of Role Conflict scores among women teachers.
2. Mean, median or $P_{50}$, $P_{75}$, $P_{25}$ were determined to find out the incidence of Role Conflict among women teachers.
3. Product moment coefficient of correlation was employed to find out the Socio-phychological correlations of Role Conflict among women teachers.

4. "t" Test was used to find out the significance of difference between mean scores of Role Conflict with respect to demographic variables.

## MAIN FINDINGS

### Major Aspects

*(a)* The distribution of Role Conflict Scores among women teachers.

*(b)* Incidence of Role Conflict among women teachers.

*(c)* Correlation between Role Conflict and Personality Factors among women teachers.

*(d)* Correlation between Role Conflict and Personality Factors with respect to demographic variables.

*(e)* Correlation between Role Conflict and Socio-economic Status of women teachers.

*(f)* Comparison of Role Conflict among women teachers with respect to demographic variables.

*(g)* Comparison of *(i)* Inter-family Role Conflict, *(ii)* Intra-family Role Conflict among women teachers with respect to demographic variables.

*(h)* Comparison of *(i)* Inter-job Role Conflict and, *(ii)* Intra-job Role Conflict among women teachers with respect to demographic variables.

*(i)* Comparison of inter-family Role Conflict and intra-family Role Conflict among women teachers with respect to demographic variables.

*(j)* Comparison of inter job Role Conflict and intra-job Role Conflict among women teachers with respect to demographic variables.

The distribution of Role Conflict scores among women teachers is normal.

Conscientious (G), Venturesome (H), Suspicious (L), Self-sufficient ($Q_2$), Controlled ($Q_3$), Humble (E), Women teachers experience high Role Conflict. It is also found that troubled (O) and reserved (A) women teachers experience high intra-role conflict. The study also shows that less intelligent (B) women teachers experience high Role Conflict.

The study also shows that sober (F) and relaxed ($Q_4$) women teachers belonging to joint family experience high Role Conflict. The findings of the study support that self-sufficient ($Q_2$) and tense ($Q_4$) women teachers with less than five years of teaching experience are prone to high Role Conflict.

Women teachers belonging to upper lower class of Socio-economic Status experience high Role Conflict.

Comparison of Role Conflict among women teachers shows that married women teachers experience high Role Conflict and unmarried women teachers experience the lowest Role Conflict. Teaching experience also affects a lot the Role Conflict faced by women teachers. It also suggests that women teachers belonging to nuclear family experience more Role Conflict in comparison to women teachers belonging to joint family. The study also reveals that married women teachers experience more inter-family Role Conflict than unmarried women teachers. It also suggests that women teachers working in private schools experience more inter-family Role Conflict than those working in aided schools. The study also reveals that women teachers with respect to various demographic variables such as J.B.T./B.Ed. married/unmarried, rural/urban, nuclear family/joint family, more than five years/less than five years of teaching experience, government schools/aided schools/ private schools, and girls schools/boys schools/co-educational schools experience more intra-job Role Conflict than inter-job Role Conflict.

## EDUCATIONAL IMPLICATIONS

The Role Conflict Scale constructed and standardised by the investigator can serve as a potential measure in the field of conflict management. The findings of the study signify that women teachers working in urban areas face more Role Conflict. So to reduce their Role Conflict a more cooperative environment must be developed in the urban schools.

The results suggest that joint family system should be encouraged as far possible.

Private institutions should be encouraged to strengthen their financial conditions by raising funds through organising other social activities so that the salaries to the teachers of such schools can be increased.

## SUGGESTIONS FOR FURTHER STUDY

1. Effect of other variables like number of children, number dependents, teacher competency, age, self concept, job satisfaction and life satisfaction in relation to Role Conflict can be explored among working women including women teachers also.
2. Comparative studies on correlates of Role Conflict among working and non-working women can be conducted.
3. Role Conflict can also be studied in relation to Role Conflict resolution system.
4. It may be suggested that there is a need of deeper probing into the problem. An interview of the family members, parents-in-iaws, neighbours, employer of working women including women teachers will be very useful.

# Bibliography


Abdel-Halim, Ahmad, A., Employee Effective Responses to Organizational Stress : Moderating Effects of Job Characteristics, in *Personnel Psychology,* (Illinois State U.) Vol. 31(3), 1978 (Feb.), pp. 561-579.

Abdulmatlub, Mohammad, A., "Labour Force Participation, Occupational distribution and Occupational Attainment of Women in Libyan Arab Jamahiriya Society", *Dissertation Abstracts International,* Vol. 52, No. 4, 1991 (Oct.), p. 19.

Abraham, M. Francis, *Modern Sociological Theory, Delhi Oxford Uni. Press,* 1986, p. 126.

Aggarwal, Y.P., *Statistical Methods,* New Delhi : Sterling, 1986.

Jung, Anees, About Women, by Women, Saturday Plus, *Hindustan Times,* Dec. 29, 1990, p. 4.

Angrist, Shirley S. and Almquist Elizabeth M., *Careers and Contingencies,* University Press of Cambridge, New York, Mass Series 1975, pp. 195-199.

Ahrentzen, Sherry, B., *Home as a Workplace in the Lives of Women, Human Behaviour and Environment : Advances in Theory and Research,* Wisconsin U., Vol. 12, 1992, pp. 113-138.

Ashraf, K.M., *Life and Conditions of the People of Hindustan,* Navchetan Press, Delhi, 1970, pp. 1-6.

Behl, Taru, Is Marriage Malaise for Working Women, *Sunday Tribune,* March, 22, 1992, p. 3.

Baig, Tara, Ali, *India's Women Power,* Delhi, S. Chand and Co. Pvt. Ltd., 1976, pp. 1-4.

Bali, S.S., *A Study of Common Personality Factors of Highly Creative Persons in Different Fields,* Ph.D. Edu. K.U.K. 1981.

Balse, Mayah, *The Indian Female : Attitude Towards Sex,* Delhi, Chetna Publications, 1976, pp. 3-7.

Bando, Mariko, Sugahra, Japanese Women : Indo Japan Relations; Pillars of Society—*The Hindustan Times,* Col. 5th, 1990, Nov. 12th.

Barber, R.E., *Marriage and Family,* New York : McGraw Hill Book Company, Inc. 1953, p. 332.

Barcinas, Jeff, David, Tainatonago, "Comparison of Attributes of Rural and Urban Secondary Schools and Twelfth Grade Students in Ohio". Ph.D. Thesis, The Ohio State University 1989, p. 336, *Dissertation Abstracts International,* Vol. 51, Number 1, 1990 (July), p. 130.

Barnabas, J., *The Central Institute of Research and Training in Public Cooperation,* New Delhi, Social Welfare, 1966 (Dec.).

Barnett, Rosalind C. and Marshall, Nancy L. (Wellesley Coll., Ctr. for Research on Women, M.A.) "Worker and Mother Roles, Spillover Effects, and Psychological Distress, Women and Health", *Psychological Abstracts,* Vol. 18 (2), 1992, pp. 9-20.

Barnett, Rosalind C. and Marshall Nancy L. (Wellesley Coll. Ctr. for Research on Women, Wellesley, M.A.). "The Relationship Between Women's Work and Family Roles and Their Subjective Well being and Psychological Distress". Plenum Press : New York, NY 1991, X p. 271, ISBN 0-306-43780-5. *Psychological Abstracts* Vol. 79, No. 4, April, 1992).

Barnett, R., and Baruch (1985), "Women's Involvement in Multiple Roles and Psychological Distress", *Journal of Applied Psychology,* Vol. 77, No. 3, June 1992, p. 274.

Bauton, Michael, *Roles—An Introduction to the Study of Social Relations,* Tavistoch Publications, London, 1965, pp. 167-170.

Bell, W. Norman and Ezra F. Vogel, *A Modern Introduction to The Family,* The Free Press, New York, 1968, p. 391.

Belok, Michael, V., *Women's and Educational Biography,* Anu Books, Meerut, 1987, pp. 1-7.

Best, John, W. and Khan, James, V., *Research in Education* Ed. 5, New Delhi, Prentice-Hall of India, 1986, pp. 46-50.

Bhoite, A., "A Study of the Problems of Employed Women in Rural Areas", *Indian Dissertation Abstracts,* Vol. 14, (1985), pp. 298-300.

Biswas, A. and Aggarwal, J.C., *Encyclopaedic Dictionary and Directory of Education,* Vol. 1, Academic Publishers, Delhi 5, 1971, p. 3.

Blank, Leonard, *Psychology for Everyday Living,* Mayflower Book, New York, 1980, pp. 133-135.

Blumberg, Rhoda, Lois, and Dwarki, Leela, *India's Educated Women : Options and Constraints,* Hindustan Publishing Corporation, Delhi, 1980.

Borg, Mark, G. and Riding, Richard, J., "Teacher Stress and Cognitive Style", *British Journal of Educational Psychology,* Printed in Great Britain, Vol. 63, 1993, pp. 271-286.

Bowman, M.A., *Marriage for Moderns* (3rd ed.), New York : McGraw Hill Book Company, 1954, pp. 7-9.

Brar J., Singh, and Om, Odhar, "The Socio-Economic Problems of Primary School teachers", *Journal of Educational Research and Extension,* Vol. 8, No. 4, April 1972.

Burke, R. and Green Class, E. Work and Family. In C. Copper and I. Robertson (Eds.) *International Review of Industrial Organization Psychology* 1987, pp. 273-320.

Burke, R. (1982), "Impact of Occupational Demands on Non-work Experiences of Senior Administrators, *Journal of Applied Psychology*", Vol. 77, No. 3, June 1992, pp. 274-278.

Butler, Sandra & Wistram, Clarie, (U. Leicester, Lecturer in Social Work, Leicester England) "Feminist Group Work Gender & Psychology", Sage Publications, Inc. London England 1991, ISBN *Psychological Abstracts,* Vol. 79, NO. 5, May 1992, p. 200.

Caplan, Robert D., Psychological Stress in Work, Management & Labour Studies (Michigan Uni., Institute for Social Research), *International Journal Abstracts.* Vol. 10(2), April 1985, pp. 63-76.

Carpenter, Jill, Linda, *"The Employment and Career Situation of Women, age 40 and Older, who have Received Services from a Rural Displaced Homemaker Programme"*, Oregon State University, Ph. D. Thesis, 1989, p. 199.

Cedraschi, C., Rossel, F. & Merceron, C., "False Self : Personality or Defence? Comparative Study of Rorschach Protocols" *British Journal of Projective Psychology,* Vol. 36 (1), June 1991, pp. 35-39.

Chilman, Catherine, S. Parental, "Employment and Child Care Trends". Some Critical Issues and Suggested Policies, *Journal of the National Association of Social Workers,* Vol. 38, No. 4, July 1993, pp. 451-460.

Chakraborty, K., *Some Variables in Role Conflict Analysis*— The Case of Middle Class Working Mothers, Sociologia Indica 1 (182), 1977, pp. 37-47.

Chaurasia, G., *Education and Status of Teachers.* Alums, Vol. 1 (13), 1966, pp. 4-11.

Chauhan, S.S., *Advanced Educational Psychology,* Delhi : Vikas Publications Pvt. Ltd., 1978, pp. 218-240.

Coleman, Malcolm, James, "The Relationship Between Job Satisfaction and Personality Traits Among Music Teachers". North Texas State University 1987, *Dissertation Abstracts International,* Vol. 48, No. 7, January 1988.

Cooper, Cary, I & Davidson, Marilyn J. (Victoria U. of Manchester, Inst. of Sciences and Technology, England). "The High Cost of Stress of Women Managers : Organizational Dynamics", Vol. 10 (4), September, 1982, pp. 44-53.

Cormack, Margaret, *The Hindu Women,* Bombay, Asia Publishing House, 1961.

Covin, Teresa J. & Brush, Christina, C. Kennesaw State Coll,

School of Business, Marietta GA "An Examination of Male and Female Attitudes Towards Career and Family Issues : Sex Roles", Vol. 25 (7-8), October, 1991, *Psychological Abstracts*, Vol. 79, No. 5, May 1992.

Dasgupta Kalpana, *Women on the Indian Scene*, Delhi, Abhinav Publications, 1976, pp. 1-10.

Das, Ira and Mathur, Reena, "Need Achievement as Related to Type A/B Behaviour Patterns Among Working and Non-Working Women". *Indian Journal of Clinical Psychology*, Vol. 19, No. 1, March 1992, pp. 18-22.

Desai, M.M., *Economic Opportunities for Women*, Social Welfare XXII (6-7), pp. 25-26.

Devi U. Lalitha, *Status and Employment of Women in India*, B.R. Publishing Corporation, Delhi, 1982, pp. 9-11.

Dhillon S. Kaur, *Study of Role Conflict in Working Women*, M.Sc. Thesis in Rural Sociology H.A.U. Hisar, 1981, pp. 1-7.

Driscoll, Michael, P., and Hildreth, K. and Ilgen Danien, "Time Devoted to Job and Off-Job Activities, Inter Role Conflict and Affective Experience", *Journal of Applied Psychology* Vol. 77, 1992, pp. 272-279.

Eichinger, Joanner; Heifetz, Louis J. & Ingraham, Chrys, (California State Uni., San Bernardino) "Situational Shifts in Sex Role Orientation : Correlates of Work Satisfaction and Burn Out Among Women in Special Education, Sex Roles". Vol. 25, October 1991 (7-8), *Psychological Abstracts* Vol. 79, No. 4 May 1992.

Floud, J., Teaching in the Affluent Society, *British Journal of Sociology*, XIII, 1962, pp. 299-307.

Fontana, D. and Abouserie, R., Stress Levels, Gender and Personality Factors in Teachers", *British Journal of Educational Psychology*, Printed in Great Britain, Vol. 63, 1993, pp. 261-270.

Frommer, Michael S; Edye Beryl V; Mandryk, John A; Grammeno, Gabrielle L. *et. al.* (National Occupational

Health and Safety Commission, Sydney, Australia), "Symbolic Blood Pressure in Relation to Occupation and Perceived Work Stress". *Scandinavian Journal of Work, Environment and Health,* Vol. 12(5), 1986, pp. 476-485.

Gage, N.L., *Handbook of Research on Teaching,* Chicago, R and McNally and Co., 1965, p. 725.

Ganser, Thomas Maurice, "The Influence of Teaching Experience on the Conceptualization of Good Teaching Among Five Beginning High School Teachers". Ed. D. The University of Wisconsin Milwankee, *Dissertation Abstracts International,* Vol. 50, Number 12, Part I, June 1990, pp. 3922-A.

Garrett M.E., *Statistics in Psychology and Education,* Vakils Feffer & Simson Pvt. Ltd., p. 340.

Gautama R.N., *"A Sociometric Study of the Patterns of Social Interaction Among Principals, Teachers and Students in Higher Secondary Schools of Himachal Pradesh"*. Ph.D. Edu. Pan. U. 1974.

Gayatri, *Vibhin Vyavsayarat Mahilaon Ka Sivaprataya"* (Self Concpet of Women in Different Occupations), Ph.D. Psy. Khasi Vidyapeeth, Varanasi, 1980.

Gillespie, Betty, L. & Eisler, Richard M., *"Development of the Feminine Gender Role Stress Scale"* : A Cognitive Behavioural Measure of Stress, Appraisal and Coping for Women. Behaviour Modifications and Coping for Women. July 1992, Vol. 16(3), *Psychological Abstracts,* Vol. 80 (1), January 1992, pp. 426-438.

Ginsberg, E. and Associates, *Life Styles of Educated Women,* New York : Columbia University Press, 1967, p. 10.

Ghosh, S.K., "Indian Women Through Ages : An Article on Women for Slavery and Sale", *The Tribune,* Dec. 29, 1990.

Ghadially, R., and Kumar, P., "Stress, Strain and Coping Styles of Female Professionals", *Indian Journal of Applied Psychology,* Vol. 26 (1) 1989, pp. 1-8.

Glass, Jennifer & Valerie, C. (U. Notre Dame, IN) Gender,

"Parenthood and Job-family Compatibility" *American Journal of Sociology*, Vol. 98 (1), July, 1992, pp. 131-151.

Goffman, E. Asylums, In G. Lindzey and Arouson, E. (1961a), The Handbook of Social Psychology, Amerind Publishing Co. Pvt. Ltd., Vol. I, 1968, pp. 560-561.

Goldberg, Wendy, A., Greenberger, Ellen Hamill Sharon & O'Neil, Robin (U. California, Programme in Social Ecology, Irvine), "Role Demands in the Lines of Employed Single Mother with Pre-Schoolers", *Journal of Family Issues*, Vol. 13 (3), Sept., 1992, pp. 312-333.

Goode, W.S., A Theory of Role Strain, *American Sociological Review*, 25, 1960, pp. 483-496.

Goode J. William, *Foundations of Modern Sociology Series*, New Delhi, Prentice-Hall of India (Private) Ltd., pp. 2-6.

Goode, W.J., *World Resolution and Family Patterns*, London. The Free Press of Glance, 1963, p. 72.

Gopal, Ram, *A Study of Role Conflict and Its Effect on Role Performance of Extrovert and Introvert Senior Secondary School Teachers of Delhi University*, Ph.D. Thesis, Meerut, University, 1987.

Gore, M.S., *Urbanisation and Family Change*, Bombay : Popular Prakashan, 1968, pp. 12-13.

——, *Urbanisation and Family Change*, Bombay : Popular Prakashan, 1968, pp. 156-173.

Gorwaney, Naintara, *Self Image and Social Change*, Delhi Sterling Publishers Pvt. Ltd., 1977, pp. 5-17.

Gough, H.G., A Sociological Theory of Psychopathy, *American Journal of Sociology*, 53, 1948, pp. 359-366. (Quoted from the Handbook of Social Psychology, 2nd Eds. Edited by Gardner Lindzey and Elliort Aronson), Vol. One, Amerind Publishing Co. Pvt. Ltd., New York, 1954.

Grace G.R. & Paul Kegan, Role Conflict and the Teacher, *The British Journal of Sociology*, Vol. 25, 1974, p. 130.

Green Cynthia P., "Age Differences Between Spouses & Status

of Women". The American Univ. *Dissertation Abstracts International*, Vol. 48, No. 7, 1987, p. 2462.

Greenhaus, Jeffrey H. & Parasuraman, Saroj (Drexel U.), "A Work-nonwork Interactive Perspective of Stress and Its Consequences—Special Issue : Job Stress : From Theory to Suggestion", *Journal of Organizational Behaviour Management*, (Fal-Win) Vol. 82 (2), 1986, pp. 37-60.

Guilford, J.P., *Psychometric Methods*, New Delhi : McGraw-Hill Publishing Co. Ltd., pp. 232-250.

——, *Psychometric Methods*, Tokyo : McGraw-Hill Book Company Ltd., p. 104.

——, *Fundamental Statistics in Psychology and Education*, New York : McGraw Hill, 1965, pp. 580-581.

Gupta, Giriraj, *Family and Social Change in Modern India* Delhi : Vikas Publishing House Pvt., Ltd. 1976.

Gupta, K. and Nisha, B., "A Study of Job Satisfaction Among Secondary School Teachers", *Asian Journal of Psycholgoy and Education*, Vol. 4 (1), 1978, pp. 25-30.

Gupta, N.S., *Organisation : Theory and Behaviour*, pp. 310-339.

Gupta, M.D., *A Study of the Status of Secondary School Teachers in Eastern U.P.*, Ph.D. Edu. BHU, 1978.

Gupta, S., *A Comparative Study of Socio-Economic Background Problems and Professional Behaviour of Men and Women Teachers in Co-Educational Institutions at Different Levels in Haryana*, Ph.D. Edu., KUK, 1981.

Gupta, V., *A Critical Study of Social and Economic Conditions of Secondary School Women Teachers and Their Relations to Their Professional Efficiency*, M.Ed. Dissertation, Jabalpur, 1958.

Gutck, B., Searle S., & Klepa, L., "Rational V. Gender Role Explanation for Work-Family Conflict", *Journal of Applied Psychology*; Vol. 76, 1991, pp. 560-568.

Guyton, John, William, "A Comparison of the Personality Traits of Secondary Science Teachers in Mississippi Public

School", Mississippi Status Univ. 1987, III Edu. D. *Dissertation Abstracts Interational*, Vol. 48, No. 10, April 1988, p. 132.

Hall, D.T. and Gorden, F.E., "Self Image and Streotype of Feminity : Their Relationship to Women's Role Conflict and Coping", *Journal of Applied Psycholgy*, 59(2), 1974, pp. 241-243.

Hamilton, Mary, Ann., "Women, Work and Family : Ways to Well Being", Virginia Polytechnic Institute and State University, 1990, p. 90, Chair : Gloria W. Bird, *Dissertation Abstracts International*, The Humanities and Social Sciences, Vol. 52, Number 1, July 1991.

Hans, Nanki, Fair Sex Thrice Burdened, An Article, *The Tribune*, January, 1993.

Harris, Diane & Brown Ric (San Fransico State U. CA) Selecting Teaching as a Profession", *College Student Journal*, Vol. 26 (2), June 1992, pp. 248-252.

Hate, C.A., *Changing Status of Women* Bombay : Allied Publishers Pvt. Ltd., pp. 1-10.

Hatta, Takeshi & Nishiide, Sachiy, (Osaka U. of Education, Japan) Teachers" Stress in Japanese Primary Schools : Comparison with Workers in Private Companies, Stress Medicine, Vol. 7 (4), Oct., Dec. 1991, pp. 207-211.

Hawes, Gene, R. and Hawes, Lynne, S., *The Concise Dictionary of Education*, USA VanNostrand Reinhold Company, 1982, pp. 208-246.

Holahan, C.K. and Gilbert L.A., "Inter Role Conflict for Working Women : Careers Vs. Jobs", *Journal of Applied Psychology*, 64 (1), 1979, pp. 86-90.

Hojat, M., "Loneliness as a Function of Selected Personality Variables", *Journal of Clinical Psychology*, Vol. 38 (1), January 1982, pp. 137-141.

Hota, S., *Working Women's Perception of Their Self and Environment in Relation to Job and Life Satisfaction*, Ph.D. Thesis, Department of Education, KUK, 1990, pp. 3-4.

Idrisi, Saeed Ahmad, *A Study of Teaching Efficiency of Teachers in Relation to Their Locality, Sex, Grade, Experience and Level of Education,* Dissertation M.Ed. Rohilkhand University, Bareilly, (UP) 1987.

Iwawkie, S. and *et al.*, "Japanese and English Personality Structure : A Cross-Cultural Study", *An International Journal of Psychology in the Orient,* Vol. 23 (4), 1980, pp. 195-205.

Jindal, B.D., "Conflict Resolution Behaviour and Commitment to Organization : A Survey Study of Teachers Perception in the College of Haryana", *Monograph,* KUK, 1990.

Jones, E.E. and Gerad, H.B., *Foundations of Social Psychology,* New York : Wiley, 1967.

Johnson, F.A. and Johnson C.L., "Role Strain in High Commitment Career Women", *Journal of the American Psycho Analysis,* 4 (1), 1976, pp. 13-36.

Kabir, Humayun, *Education in New India,* London George Allen and Unwin Ltd., 1961, pp. 153-158.

Kahn, R.L., Wolfe, O.M., Quinn, R.P., Snock J.D. and Rosenthal R.A. *et al. Organizational Stress : Studies in Role Conflict and Ambiguity,* New York : Wiley, 1964.

Kakkar, Ved, *A Study of Job Satisfaction Relation to Attitudes, Job Values and Vocational Interests of Women,* Ph.D. Edu. Bhopal Uni., 1983.

Kalhan, P., "Working Women in India : Their Probelms, *Weekly Round Table,* New Delhi, May 21, 1972.

Kalia, K., *Women : Women for Slavery and Sale.* In '*The Tribune*' Dec. 29, 1990.

Kamini, K.R., *Psycho-Social Correlates of Language Creativity Among High School Students,* M. Phil Dissertation Submitted to KUK August 1988, pp. 9-10.

Kapur, P., *Changing Status of Working Women in India,* Delhi Vikas Publishing House, 1974.

Kapur, Promilla, *Marriage and the Working Women in India,* Delhi Vikas Publications, 1970, p. 6.

Kapur, P., *Women in the Home.* In K. Bhasin, (Ed.), "The Position of Women in India", Bombay : Friedrich-Nauman Stiflong, 1972, pp. 9-12.

Kaul, L., Factorial Study of Certain Personality Variables of Popular Teachers in Secondary Schools, Ph.D. Thesis Ed. D. KUK, 1972, pp. 13 & 76.

Kerlinger, F.N., *Foundations of Behavioural Research,* New York : Holt Rinehart and Winston, Inc. 1973, pp. 1-7.

Kniveton Bromley H. (Loughborough U. of Technology England). "An Investigation of Factors Contributing to Teacher's Job Satisfaction School Psychology International", Vol. 12 (4), November, 1991, pp. 361-371. *Psychological Abstracts,* Vol. 70, No. 4, April, 1992.

Koberg, Christine S. & Chusmir & Leonard H. (U. Colorado, Coll of Business Administration, Boulder), "Sex Role Conflict in Sex at Typical Jobs : A Study of Female-male Differences". *Journal of Organisational Behaviour,* Vol. 12 (5), Sept., 1991, pp. 461-465.

Kukreti, B.R., "Teaching Aptitude and Successful Teachers : A Correlational Study"; *Indian Psychological Review,* Vol. 40, Nos. 5-6 May, June, 1993, pp. 7-14.

Kumar, S., "Teacher Effectiveness Among Different Groups of Teachers in Relation with Personality Traits", *A Research Journal,* Vol. XXVI No. 4, NCERT, Oct. 1991.

Kumud, P. Trivedi, *Secondary Education,* Vol. 7(4), March 1963, pp. 17-26.

Lakshmikutty, Amma T.S., *The Role Expectation of Teachers,* Unpublished Ph.D. Edu., Kerala U., 1978.

Leigh, James, H.; Lucas, George, H. & Woodman, Rechard W. *et. al.* (Texas A & MU, College Station), "Effects of Perceived Organizational Factors on Role Stress—Job Attitude Relationships", *Journal of Management,* Vol. 14 (1), March 1988, pp. 41-58.

Lindzey G. and Aronson, E., *The Handbook of Social Psychology,* Amerind Publishing Co. Pvt. Ltd. New York, 1968, pp. 488-539.

Linton, R., *The Cultural Background of Personality*, New York Appleton-Century Crafts, 1945.

———, *The Study of Man*, New York, Appleton-Century Crafts, 1936, pp. 113-114.

Lovell K. & Lawson, K.S., *Understanding Research in Education*, University of London Press Ltd., St. Paul's House Worwick Lane, London Ecy, 1970, pp. 64-69.

Lynn C. Mary, *Women's Liberation in the Twentieth Century* John Wiley & Sons Inc. (New York, London, Sydney, Toranto), U.S.A.

MacMillan, T.S. & Valliant Paul M. (Laurentian U. of Sludbury, or Canada), "Occupational Stress and Behavioural Change, Perceptual and Motor Skills", Vol. 64 (3, Pt. 2), June, 1987, pp. 1061-1062.

Mahajan, A., Women's Two Roles : A Study of Role Conflict, *Indian Journal of Social Work*, Vol. 24 (4), pp. 377-380.

Mane, P., "Women at Work : A Study of Women Employees at the Secretariat". *Indian Dissertation Abstracts*, Vol. 13, 1984, pp. 249-252.

Mann, S.S., *Correlates of Success in Teaching of Secondary School Teachers*, Unpublished Ph.D., Edu. P. Uni., 1980, pp. 7-8.

Maqsad, M., "Extraversion, Neuroticism, Intelligence and Academic Achievement in Northern Nigeria", *British Journal of Edu. Psychology*, Vol. 50 (1), February 1980, pp. 71-73.

Marihal, B.G., "Teacher and His Status : A Comparative Study", *Journal of College of Education*, Karnataka University, Vol. 5 (2), 1967, pp. 33-36.

Martin, Mary, E.R., *Women in Ancient India*, Chowkhamba Publications, 1964, pp. 1-9.

Mathur, S.S., *Educational Psychology*, Vindo Pustak Mandir Agra, 1972, pp. 1-5.

McCormick, John & Solman, Robert (U. New South Wales, School of Teacher Education, Sydney, Australia),

"Teacher's Attributions of Responsibility for Occupational Stress and Satisfaction : An Organisational Perspective." Educational Studies, 1992, Vol. 18 (2), *Psychological Abstracts,* Vol. 80, No. 1, January 1993, pp. 201-222.

McClain, Clifford, R., "The Relationship Between Personality Characteristics and Teaching Effectiveness of Secondary Vocational Agriculture Teachers", The Uni. of Nebraska Lincoln 1987, *Diss. Abs. Int.,* Vol. 48, No. 7, 1988.

Mckenry, *et. al.,* "Family and Job Influences on Role Satisfaction of Employed Rural Mothers", *Psychology of Women Quarterly,* Vol. 9 (2), 1985, pp. 242-257.

Mehta, G.L., "A Study of Role Conflicts of Teachers", Unpublished Ph.D. Edu. MSU, 1985.

Michaels, Ronald E.; Day, Ralph, L. & Joachimsthaler, Erich, A. (U. Kanas, School of Business), Role Stress Among Industrial Buyers : An Integrative Model, *Journal of Marketing,* Vol. 51 (2), April, 1987, pp. 28-45.

Miles, Robert H. (Yale U.), Role-set Configuration as a Predictor of Role Conflict and Ambiguity in Complex Organization. *Sociometry,* Vol. 40 (1), March 1977, pp. 21-34, *Journal Abstracts International,* Vol. 36 (6-B), December, 1975, 3106-3107.

Miller, Jean, Baker, *Towards a New Psychology of Women,* Allen Lane, 1976, pp. 14-131.

Mohanty P., *A Study of Organizational Commitment and Organizational Health of Secondary School Women Teachers",* Unpublished Dissertation, KUK, 1992.

Moradi, Sandra, Schoeni, "An Analysis of Workplace Conditions that Impact on Job Satisfaction Among Secondary School Teachers in South East Asia Expatriate Schools". Unpublished Ph.D., The Uni. of Iowa, 1987, *Dissertation Abstracts International,* Vol. 48, No. 10, April, 1988.

Mori, Takako, "Analysis of Factors Influencing Motivations for Becoming a Teacher", *Journal of Educational Research,* Vol. 60, December 1960, pp. 174-179.

Morris, Celia, H., "Current Well-being of Midlife Employed Women with Differential Work and Marital Histories" Ed. D. Harvard University, 1989. *Dissertation Abstracts International,* Vol. 51, No. 2, August 1990, p. 659.

Morton, Deutsch, *The Resolution of Conflict Constructive and Destructive Processes,* Yale University, New Haven, Connecticut, 1973, p. 10.

Mouley, G.J., The Science of Educational Research, New Delhi : Eurasia.

Mukthamath, G.C.; Gaokar and Khadi, Pushpa B. (Uni. of Agricultural Sciences), *Indian Journal of Behaviour,* India, July 1991, Vol. 15(3), *Psychological Abstracts,* Vol. 70, No. 4, April 1992.

Murphy, G., *An Introduction to Psychology,* Harper & Row Publishers, New York, 1951, p. 117.

———, *An Introduction to Psychology,* Oxford Book Company Harper and Row Publishers, New York, 1964, pp. 117-120.

Mutha, D., "An Attitudinal and Personality Study of Effective Teachers", Unpublished Ph.D. Thesis, Psy. Jodhpur Univ., 1980, *Indian Psychological Review,* Vol. 40, No. 5-6, 1993, p. 7.

Myrdal, Alva, & Klein, Viola, *Women's Two Roles;* Home and Work, London : Routledge & Kegan Paul Ltd., 1956, pp. 1-6.

Nair, S.R., "Academic Achievement and Social Background as Predictors of Teacher Effectiveness", *Teacher Education Journal,* Vol. VI, No. 4, July, 1962, Delhi, pp. 17-22.

Negoescu-Boder, Victoria; Olteau, Tatiana & Popa S. (National Inst. of Gerontology and Geriatrics, Bucharest, Romania), "Dimensions of Psychological Adjustment in Workers and Longevous, *Revenue Roumaine des Sciences Sociales—Serie de Psychologie*", 1990, (Jul-Dec) Vol. 34 (2), pp. 159-169, *Pscyho. Abst.,* Vol. 79, No. 3, March, 1992.

Nenslin, James, M., *Marriage and the Working Women in India* Delhi, Vikas Publications, 1970, pp. 2-4.

Nevill, D. and Demico, S., "Role Conflict in Women as a Function of Martial Status", *Human Relations,* Vol. 28 (5), 1975, pp. 487-497.

Nevill, D. and Demico, S., "Family Size and Role Conflict in Women", *Journal of Psychology,* Vol. 89 (2), 1975, pp. 267-270.

Newton, T.J. & Keenan, A. (U. Edinburgh, Scotland), "Role Stress Examined : An Investigation of Role Stress Predictors Organisational Behaviour and Human Decision Processes", *Psychological Abstracts,* Vol. 40 (3), December 1987, pp. 346-368.

Nhundu, Tichatonga Josphat, *Job Satisfaction of Teacher in terms and Its Relationship to Self Appraisals, Supervisor—Appraisals, Role Ambiguity and Selected Background Variables,* Uni. of Alberta (Canada), 1987.

Norwood Janet L., "Working Women Where have be been? Where are we going?" Population and Environment, *A Journal of Interdisciplinary Studies,* Vol. 14 (1), Sept. 1992, pp. 95-103, (Urban Inst., Washington, DC).

Nye, F.I. & Berardo F.M., *The Family Its Structure and Interaction,* London, 1980, p. 263.

Odo, Maurice G.O.C., "Principal Leadership Behaviour as Perceived by Principals and Teachers in Nigerian Secondary Schools", Uni. of San Fransisco, 1986, p. 239, *Dissertation Abstracts International,* Vol. 47, No. 9, 1987.

Organ, Dennis W. & Greens, Charles N., Indiana U. Graduate School of Business, "Role Ambiguity, Locus of Control and Work Satisfaction", *Journal of Applied Psychology,* Vol. 59(1), Feb., 1974, pp. 101-102.

Prasad, P., *Aspirations, Adjustment and Role Conflict in Primary and Secondary School Teachers,* Ph.D. Psy. Bhagalpur Uni., 1985.

Phelps, Richard, S., "Conditions of Teaching and the English Teacher : A Sociological Perspective", Ed. D. Boston Uni. 1987, *Dissertation Abstracts International,* Vol. 48, No. 7, Jan. 1988.

Poole, Millicent E. & Langan-Fox, Janice (Manash U, Faculty of Education (Layton, Vict. Australia) Conflict in Women's Decision Making About Multiple Roles, *Australian Journal of Marriage and Family*, Vol. 13 (1), March 1992, pp. 2-18.

Porwal, N.K., *Personality Correlates to Job Satisfied Hr. Sec. Sch. Teachers* Unpublished Ph.D. Psy Agra, Uni. 1980.

Quinn, Jean, Maurer, "Cognitive Style, Personality and Classroom Management of Special Education Teachers in Non-Public Schools", Claremont Public School, 1987, *Dissertation Abstracts International*, Vol. 48, No. 10, April 1988.

Rane, S.A., *An Investigation into the Self Improvement Programme of Working Mothers in Greater Bombay with a view to Examine Increased Psychological Problems in Society*, Unpublished Ph.D. Edu. Bombay U., 1986.

Rani, Kala, *Role Conflict in Working Women*, Chetna Publications, Delhi 1976, pp. 1-10.

Recommendations Concerning the Status of Teachers, Teacher in Developing Countries : A Survey of Employment Condition Geneva ILO, 1991, ISBN 92-2-106441-7, p. 137.

Reddy, C. Raghunadha, *Changing Status of Educated Working Women*, B.R. Publishing Corporation, Delhi, 1986.

*Report of the Committee on Status of Women in India*, Towards Equality, New Delhi : Department of Social Welfare, Government of India, 1974.

*Report of the Government of India*, Ministry of Labour and Employment, Women in Employment, Simla, 1964.

*Report of the Government of India*, Ministry of Labour, Labour Bureau, Economic and Social Status of Women Workers in India, 1953.

Rice, Karla, K., "Cross Cultural Work Environments, Fusions of Histories and Traditions Among Newcomer Teachers to California", Ed. D., University of San Fransico, 1990. *Dissertation Abstracts International*. The Humanities and Social Sciences, Vol. 51, No. 5, Nov. 1990, p. 1571A.

Ringuette, Eugene L. (Purdue U.), "Selected Personality Correlates of Mode of Conflict Resolution", *Journal of Personality and Social Psychology*, 2 (4), 1965, pp. 506-512.

Rtizer, G., *Man and His Work*, Conflict and Change, USA 1972, pp. 7-13.

Rtizer, George, *Man and His Work* : Conflict and Change Appleton-Century-Crofts, Educational Division, Meredith Corporation 440, Park Avenue South, New York, 1972, pp. 117-135.

Robbins, Stephen P., *Organisational Behaviour*, Prentice Hall of India Private Limited, New Delhi, 1988, pp. 292-310.

Robinson, Sharon E. & Skarie, Elizabeth K. (Arizona State U. Temple) Professional Women : Job Role Stresses and Psychological Variables *American Mental Health Counsellors Association Journal*, Vol. 8 (3), July 1986, pp. 157-165.

Rosenberg, Morris and Turner, Ralph, M., *Social Psychology*, Basic Books Inc. Publishers, New York, 1981; pp. 94-132.

Saita, P., *A Study of Role Commitments and Conflicts of Women Teachers of Thailand in Relation to Some Variables*, Unpublished Ph.D. Thesis, Edu., SPU, 1984.

Saluja, S., Boss Se Dori...Kitni Jaruri? *Sunday Dainik Tribune* (Hindi) July 19, 1992.

Santha K.C., *Changing Role of Women in Indian Society and Its Implications of Education*, Unpublished Ph.D. Edu., Madras, U., 1986.

Sarbin, T.R., *Role Theory* (Quoted from G. Lindzey (ed.), *Handbook of Social Psychology*, Cambridge Mass ; Addition Wessley, 1954.

Savery, Lawson K. (Western Australian Inst. of Technology School of Management, Bustley), "Stress and the Employee", *Journal of Leadership and Organization Development*, Vol. 7(2), 1986, pp. 17-20.

Scott, Ernestine, Hicks, *Black Professional Women in Dual*

*Career Families : The Relationship of Marital Equality and Sex Role Identity to the Career Commitment of the Wife,* Ed. D. Virginia Polytechnic Institute and State University by, 1990, p. 192.

Segal, Uma, A. (Missouri, St. Louis), "Values, Personality and Career Choice", *Journal of Applied Social Sciences,* (Spr-Sun) Vol. 16 (2), 1992, pp. 143-159.

Seidman S.A. & Zager J., "Work and Stress", *Journal of Psychology,* Vol. 5 (3), Jul-Sept., 1991, pp. 205-216.

Seidman Susan Myrna, "Work-Family Role Conflict and Marital Adjustment in Dual—Career Couples", Fordhan Uni., *Dissertation Abstract International,* Vol. 4 (3), 1989, p. 174.

Sen Gupta, Shanker, *A Study of Women of Bengal,* Calcutta Indian Publications, 1970, pp. 1-5.

Shaheen, P.A., *A Sociological Study of 300 Higher Sec. School Female Teachers in the City of Lucknow,* Unpublished Ph.D. Soc. Luc. U., 1973.

Shamsuddin, "Influence of Socio-Economic Factors on the Teachers", Career; *Indian Education Quarterly,* Vol. 7, 1986, pp. 6-7.

Sharma, A., *A Mother-Child Relationship as a Function of Family Size and Socio-Economic Status Among Working House-Wives of Meerut,* Unpublished Ph.D. Psy. Agra U., 1981.

Sharma, B.M. *Correlates of Job Satisfaction Among Skilled and Unskilled Workers,* Unpublished Ph.D. Thesis KUK 1979, pp. 39-46.

Shukla, R., "Education", *Journal of Edu. Research,* Vol. 40(10), Oct. 1961, pp. 6-11.

Sinha, P., "Some Personality Correlates of Feminine Role Concept", *Journal of Psychological Researches,* 17 (3), pp. 108-112.

Singh, I.M., *"A Comparative Study of Creative and Non-Creative B.Ed. Pupil Teachers in Relation to Teaching Effectiveness, Self Concept and Some Personal Values in M.P.,* Ph.D. in Education, Bhopal Uni., 1987.

Singh, K.P., "Career and Family, Women's Two Roles", *Indian Journal of Social Work,* Vol. 3, 1972, pp. 278-281.

Sinha, P., *Role Conflict Among the Working Women,* Patna : Janki Prakashan, 1988, pp. 110-112.

Sinha, P., *Role Conflict Among Working Women,* Janki Prakashan, Patna, New Delhi, 1988, pp. 2-5.

Som, P., "Teachers Personality Pattern and Their Attitudes Towards Teaching and Related Areas", Unpublished Ph.D. Thesis, 1984.

Srivastava, G.N.P. and Sharma, T.N., "Teaching Effectiveness and Personality Traits of Four Years and one year Teacher Trainees : A Comparative Study" *Journal of Education and Psychology,* 47 (3-4), Oct. Jan. 1989, pp. 101-109 tabs.

Steffens, Peggy, Johanne, "Characteristics of Teacher Efficacy as Perceived by Teachers of the Year", Ed. D. Northern Arizona University, 1990, *Dissertation Abstracts International,* Vol. 51, Number 12, June 1991, pp. 4092A.

Stillson, Richard W.; O'Neil, James M. & Owen, Steven V. (U. Connecticut School of Education), "Counselling Psychology Program, predictors of Adult Men's Gender Role Conflict : Race, Class, Unemployment, Age, Instrumentality Expressiveness and Personal Strain", *Dissertation Abstracts International,* Oct. Vol. 38 (4), Oct. 1991, pp. 458, 464.

Strickland, Benjain, Franklin, *A Study of Factors Effecting Teacher Morale in Selected Administrative Morals of North Carolona,* Unpublished Doctoral Thesis, 1962, p. 182.

Strickland, W. Jay. (Georgia Southern U. Stratesboro), "Institutional Emotion Norms and Role Satisfaction : Examination of a Career Wife Population", Sex Roles, May 1992, Vol. 26 (9-10), *Psychological Abstracts,* Vol. 80, No. 1, 1993 (Jan.), pp. 423-439.

Suchdev, J., Working Mothers, *An Interview Social Welfare,* 21 (2), 1974, 10-27.

Sukhwal, K.D., *Attitudes of Married Lady Teachers Towards the Teaching Profession,* Unpublished Ph.D. Thesis Edu. Udai, Uni., 1976.

Symonda P.M., "Characteristics of Effective Teachers, Based on Pupil Evaluation", *Journal of Experimental Eduction* 23, pp. 289-310.

T.V. Zee, Mummy Office Jati Hai : *A Serial;* An Interview of Children and Parents, Aug., 1993.

Thakur, T., *Working Conditions of the Married Women Teachers in the Primary Schools of Assam with Special Reference to Sibsagar District,* Ph.D. Edu., Gan. U., 1978.

Tipping, Lenore M. & Farmer, Helen, S. (U. Illinois, Urbana Champaign), "A Home-Career Conflict Measure : Career Counselling Implications", Measurement and Evaluation in Counselling and Development, Vol. 24 (3), 1991 (Oct.). *Psychological Abstracts,* Vol. 79, No. 3, 1992 (Mach), pp. 111-118.

Tiwari, I. Prabha, "Perceived Characteristics of Working Non-Working Women", *Indian Psychological Review,* Vol. 38, Nos. 8-9, 1992, pp. 20-24.

Tremaglio, Robert, Caeser, "The Relationship Among Principal Role Conflict and Ambiguity Principal Effectiveness and Teacher Morale", Ed. D. Uni. of Bridgeport, 1987, *Disser. Abs. Int.* Vol. 48, No. 7, 1988, p. 124.

Tsegga, A., *The Effects of Sex, SES and Generation on the Acculturation*", E.D. University of Southern California, 1983.

Tufan, K.S., "Najariya Badliya Bazoor", *Aangan Sunday Observer,* Feb. 21, 1992, p. 14.

Uma, R., *A Social Psychological Study of Women Teachers,* Ph.D. Psy. Osm. U., 1983.

Verghese, Jamila, *Her, Gold and Her Body,* Vikas Publishing House, U.P. (India), 1980.

Verma, L.K. & Sharma N.K., *Basic Statistics in Education and Psychology,* Jammu, Radha Krishna Anand & Co. 1984.

Verma, P.L., *Role Conflict and the Corresponding Role performance Among Headmasters,* Ph.D. Edu., Raj. Uni., 1975.

Verma, V., "Indian Women in Search of Justice", *The University Review, Jammu University Research Journal of Social Science,* Vol. IX, 1992 (July), pp. 18-19.

Vohra, Asa, Rani, *Bhartiya Non-Asmita Aur Adhikar,* New Delhi National Publications, New Delhi, 1989, pp. 120-122.

Venkata Rayappa, K.N., *Feminine Roles,* Popular Prakashan Bombay, 1966.

Vrooman, Roona, J., *Predictors of Role Conflict, Role Ambiguity and Propensity to Leave Among Academic Department Secretaries,* Ed. D., The College William and Mary, 1990.

Wadhera, R.C. Teachers Status in Society. *NIE Journal,* 6(5) Vol. 7, No. 4, 1972 (Dec.).

Ward, Barbara E., *Women in New Asia,* UNESCO, 1963.

Webster, Pamela Smith, *Sex Differences in Depression in a life Course Perspective : The Role of Paid Work Homework, Family Structure and Union Characteristics,* Uni. of Michigan, Vol. 52, No. 3. 1991 (Sept.), p. 289.

Wilson, B.R., "The Teachers Role, a Sociological Analysis, *British Journal of Sociology* XIII (1), 15-32.

Westergaard J. and Henrietta, Resler, *Women in Labour Market* Penguin, 1976, pp. 110-117.

Worsley, Peter, *Problems of Modern Society,* A Sociological Perspective, Penguin, 1976, pp. 110-117.

Yates, G. Graham, *What Women Want,* Harward University Press, US, 1975, pp. 118-121.

Yin-ling Irene Wrong Irwin Garfinkel and Sara Mclanahan, "Single Mother Families in Eight Countries, Economic Status and Social Policy", *Journal of Social Service Review,* Vol. 67, No. 2, 1993 (June), The University of Chicago.

Young, Kinball, *Personality and Problems of Adjustment,* Oxford Press, Plymouth, 1957, pp. 513-524.

# INDEX